EXPOSING THE EIGHT DEADLY STEPS IN EVERY TEMPTATION!!

"UNMASKING THE ONE WEAPON OF THE ENEMY, STEP-BY-STEP!!"

THIRD PRINTING

Elder Ralph Anthony Martino

EXPOSING THE EIGHT DEADLY STEPS IN EVERY TEMPTATION!!

"UNMASKING THE ONE WEAPON OF THE ENEMY, STEP-BY-STEP!!"

Elder Ralph Anthony Martino

PUBLISHED BY:
BRENTWOOD CHRISTIAN PRESS
4000 BEALLWOOD AVENUE
COLUMBUS, GEORGIA 31904

FOREWORD

In the book of Ecclesiastes, King Solomon informs us that: *"The thing that hath been, it is that which shall be; and that which is done is that which shall be done: and there is no new thing under the sun."*

True to this declaration, throughout all of human history, the adversary has employed the same old bag of tricks. In his attempts to destroy the Divine destiny of humanity and the sacred relationship that God intends to exist between Himself and Man, Satan has made full use of his favorite tactic: temptation. His most successful strategy is to try to persuade or entice us to do something immoral or sensually pleasurable. And the truth is that while temptation in most cases does lead to some temporary pleasure, what the devil masks are the much more lasting consequences of those actions. Countless enduring tragedies have been initiated simply because of momentary acquiescence to a meaningless temptation.

However, as great as our temptations may be, greater is the power that worketh in us. For the Lord has promised to give us power over all the power of the enemy, and one of our greatest sources of power is knowledge. When we know Satan's tactics in advance, we are better prepared to combat him. This book is one of God's blessings in that it breaks down all of the components of temptation, thereby empowering the reader to conquer temptation. God has anointed Pastor Ralph Martino to pen a book that will change the lives of all who read it. I am convinced that the principles illuminated in this book will be a blessing in the life of the reader.

Bishop Alfred A. Owens, Jr., D.Min.
Senior Pastor, Greater Mt. Calvary Holy Church
Washington, D. C.

PREFACE

What does it mean to be tempted? What is the process, the cost and the results of falling into temptation? Have you ever wondered why you fall prey to the same temptation repeatedly, seemingly unable to walk in victory in that area of your life? Do you really desire to know what a temptation is and how to overcome it? Has it ever dawned on you that there are sequential steps involved in every temptation and that if you or I could determine by the Spirit what those steps are, just maybe we could bring to a screeching halt the enemy's train of thoughts against us?

These questions and others are addressed and answered in this book, that the Spirit of GOD has authored through me to help believers comprehend with clarity the steps involved in every temptation. What a blessing to have at our fingertips a book that unmasks the modus operandi of the enemy! What an invaluable resource to make available to every believer, from the babe in Christ to the Road Scholar!

Every one of us is tempted everyday of our lives, therefore, it behooves us to know the functionality, the process, the impact and the devastation temptations can have on us if we do not arm ourselves with Biblical knowledge. If every one of us is tempted, and we know that we are, wouldn't you agree that it is high time for us to get combat ready and defeat the enemy at his game?

Friends, over the past several years, as I was led to look back over my life and see the manifold mistakes that I made, I had to contribute them to my lack of knowledge about the subject matter at hand, temptations. I fell prey so many times to the trickery and the deceitfulness of temptations, that it very easily could have cost me my life. It was out of the experiences of loss, heartache, failure, depression and low self-esteem that GOD birth this book within me, so that other believers can receive hope in their hopeless situations, help in their time of need, and healing from their past mistakes. I thank GOD for Jesus, who saved me and delivered me, so that He could place in our hands, in our hearts and in our libraries, penetrating truths that can and will deliver us from the ***one*** weapon of the enemy, temptation!

Whether we realize it or not, satan only has ***one*** weapon to use against the believer and that weapon is "temptation!" Every other act of lying, deceiving, fornicating, conniving, cheating, stealing, etc., is a result of first being tempted by the enemy. Just think about it for a moment! We have been trying to destroy the fruit of temptations instead of uprooting the source of temptations. Satan is quite upset right now, because for the first time the Spirit of the Lord has revealed his ***one*** weapon in eight steps to the believer, which will enable the believer to see right through his smoke screen of temptations. On numerous occasions the enemy has tried to attack my family and me and has tried to derail this anointed project from the Heavenly Father, but thanks be unto GOD for His grace and mercy, which enabled us to fight the good fight of faith and finish the course!

I thank GOD for this Soldier's Manual, which teaches us step-by-step, how over the years in my life and yours, the enemy has led us astray and seized from us our joy, peace and prosperity. But now, by the Grace of GOD, we shall walk in victory! We shall walk in righteousness! We shall walk in holiness! We shall live in prosperity, spirit, soul and body, because we have in our hands, delivered out of the enemy's camp, the highly confidential, top secret, "for his eyes only", classified documents, which reveal his strategies and tactics against the believer! Praise GOD!

According to the Biblical definition of temptation, only those who have been born again can be tempted. Those who are born once possess the Adamic or fleshly nature and are the children of satan, therefore he does not have to tempt them, he leads or drives them. But the believer, who is in Christ, satan, through whatever means necessary, must tempt them to step out of Christ. As you study to show yourself approved and read this book under the unction of the Holy Spirit, we pray that the eyes of your understanding be enlightened and that revelation knowledge flows into your innermost being with power and conviction.

If you truly desire to walk in the Spirit, then a thorough understanding of the contents in this book becomes necessary. If you truly desire to live by the Spirit, then feast your spirit on the words in this manual. If you earnestly desire to prosper and take back that which the enemy has stolen from you, then equip yourself with this life changing knowledge. If you are tired of falling into the same rut over and over again, meditate on these truths and watch the Holy Spirit teach you and reveal to you your way of escape during each step.

This book has helped to revolutionize my life and the lives of countless others. We believe and pray that your victory or victories are just pages away! We invite you now to read and share in what we believe to be a Holy Spirit inspired book that will glorify GOD, edify the Saints and horrify satan! GOD Bless you!

ACKNOWLEDGEMENTS AND DEDICATION

First and foremost, I would like to thank GOD the Father, GOD the Son and GOD the Holy Spirit for making this vision a reality. Without them I can do nothing!

I thank GOD for my Mother whose continued, fervent prayers for me helped me to overcome the challenges of life that tried to destroy me.

I thank GOD for my Wife and family, who have prayed and fasted for me during the writing and publishing of this manuscript. Drenna, Olivia, Elizabeth, mom and dad, thank you for allowing me the time, coupled with the peace and quiet necessary to write under the anointing.

I thank GOD for my brothers and sisters who have eagerly and lovingly supported me with their prayers throughout my life and ministry.

I thank GOD for all of the mentors: Bishop Alfred Owens, Bishop Alonzo Jones, Rev. Dr. Luther M. Bailey, and others who He placed in my life who have positively influenced me to achieve excellence in ministry.

I thank GOD for all of my friends and students who sat under this teaching and were a blessing to me in ministry.

I thank GOD for my Church families who have supported me. You will always have a special place in my heart.

And I thank GOD for you the reader, who has taken the step of faith in acquiring this book. May GOD richly bless you and keep you!

CONTENTS

Chapter One
What is a Temptation?

❖ What is a temptation? An act or condition which tempts or tests.

This book is a course study on temptation. Each day we live and breathe, temptation is present. We are ***all*** vulnerable to temptation. There are no exceptions as the test is sure.

Temptation often whispers, knocks or explodes on the scene without warning or respect of persons. Without warning? How then can we predict and prevail in the midst of an attack? Preparedness. If we *know* that an unwelcome caller will knock at our doors at any given hour of every day, then we have a clue and an option to reject the call. Satan is the enemy of every believer and non-believer, and his approach is relentless. Satan knocks for no other reason than to tempt us for evil, hoping that we will yield to him to achieve his ultimate goal – separation from God. Given the constant threat, we would do well to guard ourselves 24-7 against opening the door to the enemy as he consistently peeps, knocks and pounds us with temptation in our lives. "For we wrestle not against flesh and blood, but against principalities, against powers, against the rulers of the darkness of this world, against spiritual wickedness in high places" (Eph. 6:12). The Bible instructs all believers to seek divine protection when embattled by spiritual warfare. "Put on the whole armour of God, that ye may be able to stand against the wiles of the devil" (Eph. 6:11).

Think about it. A temptation is an act or condition which tempts or tests. What is the key to passing any test? Preparation. When we thoroughly study the subject matter and recall pertinent knowledge at the time of examination, then we pass the test with high marks. So then, should we *study* temptation in order to pass the test when it comes? Absolutely! While satan tempts us by shuffling his plays and players, the process or cycle of temptation is deliberate, repetitive and predictable. As we familiarize ourselves with satan's eight deadly steps in temptation, we prepare ourselves for victory!

Is temptation a new thing? Of course not. In the beginning, the serpent (the embodiment of satan) tempted Adam and Eve in the Garden of Eden (Genesis 3). We will examine the actions of Brother Adam and Sister Eve throughout this book. However, is satan the only tempter or tester? No. Believers test God to confirm His will. The Pharisees tempted God by desiring to put a yoke on the disciples' necks (Acts 15:10). Do you remember Gideon? He tested God by placing a dry fleece on the ground. Gideon asked God to moisten the fleece with dew and to leave the surrounding earth completely dry. Gideon wanted to test God to confirm His will for his life – whether he was called to deliver Israel. What did God do? He manifested his power to Gideon who later found the earth around the fleece dry, and so much dew on the fleece he was able to wring a bowl full of water from it. Gideon sought further confirmation. He asked God to reverse the phenomenon – to leave the fleece dry atop dew covered earth. God answered Gideon's second test by producing a bone dry fleece atop dewy earth (Judges 6:37-40).

Satan tempts man and man tests God. Man is also tested by God. God, who is omniscient, requires no confirmation in order to know our will toward Him. God tests us to qualify, certify and approve us as believers. God tests believers in order to reveal and prove what is within man's nature (Deut. 8:2,3) and to prove what comes out of man's character (Gal.

5:19-23). God also tests us to reveal to *us* our place in Him for His glory. Abraham is a powerful and wonderful example of an Old Testament character who was tested to sacrifice his only son, Isaac (Gen. 22:1-14; Heb. 11:17-19). Abraham was tried, tested and tempted by Jehovah to prove himself faithful to Him in all things, not just in a few things. God tried Abraham with the known expectation that he would pass the test, and bring glory to His name and disgrace to the name of satan. God never tempts or tests us for the purpose of evil because He is holy! (I Peter 1:15,16) Also, be assured that God does not tempt man to sin, because He is righteous! (Psalm 7:9) On the other hand, satan never uses temptation to approve the believer. Satan's goal is to tempt and disapprove the believer's position and practice in Christ, and to slander God's name.

The area of concentration for this book is satan's temptation against mankind. By the grace of God, we will expose the reality and predictability of satan's temptations. Unlike the temptations of man testing God, or God testing man, satan always tempts us to commit sin. We will focus on temptation that solicits us to commit evil works, speak evil words and think evil thoughts. "Let no man say when he is tempted, I am tempted of God: for God cannot be tempted with evil, neither tempteth He any man: But every man is tempted when he is drawn away of his own lust, and enticed" (James 1:13-14). This Scripture qualifies for us the subjective (internal) source of temptations. Satan's goal is to provoke a visceral reaction within us by tempting us with objective (external) sources originating in the flesh and the world system. These external sources appeal to the very core of our own lusts or sinful nature. The enemy has no scruples. Satan tempted the fallen angels (II Peter 2:4; Rev. 12:3,4). He not only tempted Adam, the federal head of

God's original creation, but also Jesus, the federal head of God's new creation. We should note that God sees man either in Adam or in Christ. Adam represents the old creation lost in sin and under the wrath of God. Christ represents the new creation, clothed in righteousness and justified by the blood of Jesus. In I Corinthians 15:22, 45-50, the Apostle Paul, under the inspiration of the Holy Spirit, reveals this great truth of being in Adam or in Christ.

Now let's return to the original question. What is a temptation? Webster defines temptation as "the act of tempting or the state of being tempted especially to evil: ENTICEMENT". The Greek words, *dokimazo* and *periazo*, are found in the New Testament. *Dokimazo* means "to test or prove a thing whether it is worthy to be received or not; by implication, to approve, to prove, to try". Similarly, *Periazo* means "tempt, a putting to proof (by experiment of good), experiencing evil, solicitation, discipline or provocation; by implication, adversity". Both Greek renderings of the word convey the definition and idea of "testing" or "temptation". Believers are always tested and tried by life's circumstances. Spiritual survival is determined by how effectively we respond when we are challenged and tried by the frailties and weaknesses of our flesh. Let's further examine the meaning of temptation and what it means to be tempted.

Temptations are instigated conflicts, initiated by external or internal forces, which create guerilla warfare between the desires of the old man and the new man.

> Temptations can result in yielding to sinful desires built or programmed into the mind and heart of man by satan, some other outside influence or from our own lusts (James 1:13-14). These desires produce

sinful words, "for out of the abundance of the heart the mouth speaks" (Matt.12:34). Corrupt desires flow from evil thoughts that proceed from the evil heart or nature of man (Mark 7:21-23). Satan programs the believer as the systems engineer programs code into computer software. The deceiver "installs" his "purpose, plans and promises" package into our souls while he simultaneously runs an "uninstall" of God's "purposes, plans and promises". The result is the virus stricken hard drive of our soul, with all traces of truth, hope and love erased. Beware of satan's path of destruction!

Evil thoughts lead to immoral desires, which lead to sinful acts or behavior (Prov. 23:7; Rom. 8:5; Matt. 15:19). These thoughts manifest a sinful, fleshly character (Gal. 5:19-21), which form sinful habits (Rom. 7:14-23), promote an immoral lifestyle (Gal. 6:8; James 5:5), and result in a doomed eternal destiny (I Cor. 6:9-10). Catering to the flesh yields only short term rewards, unworthy of banishment from the bliss of communing with God for all eternity! (Matt. 7:21-23; 25:30)

Temptations are the means by which satan seeks to resurrect the old man, rehire the body of sin, and enthrone sin as master once again. Romans 6:6 reveals to us that the cross of Christ crucified the old man, annulled (made void) the body of sin, and dethroned sin as master. Through temptation, satan attempts to undue what the cross of Christ completed. Satan's desire is to leave believers ignorant and without spiritual knowledge of the power we have through Christ to overcome temptation.

Satan is well aware that he AND his temptations are rendered powerless against the new man, the Christ controlled believer! Oh yes! The devil and his wiles are instantly defeated by the matchless name of Jesus, Hallelujah! Satan knows he must bring back to life the old creation in the believer in order to operate in the earth. He can only function through the flesh, and not man's quickened human spirit.

Temptations are the means by which satan seeks to seize our senses, paralyze our thinking processes, freeze up our emotions and capture our wills, thus hindering the work of God to advance his own plan. Satan must capture our wills before he can cut us off from the supply of the Spirit, rendering us weak to our flesh and subject to his desires.

Temptations are strategic ploys initiated by satan for his advantage over the believer. He wants to render us hypocrites in the Kingdom of God. Satan delights in deceiving the very elect of God. He wants us to remain carnal minded, and to behave as if God's Word and Spirit are powerless to overcome our flesh. Satan's ultimate goal is to turn our victories and testimonies into a mere mockery, to damage God's witness in the earth, and to dishonor and disgrace the character of Christ and Christianity as a whole.

What does it mean *to be tempted*? To be tempted is to be enticed by something or some person to commit an unwise or immoral act, especially by a promise of reward. To beguile or draw into a wrong or foolish course of action, to allure, to entice, to seduce. The following words have been extracted from Webster's Dictionary, Vine's Expository Dictionary and Strong's Concordance for the purpose of further illuminating the meaning of being tempted:

Allure: to tempt with something or someone desirable, to tempt or fascinate. (*See* Hosea 2:14; II Peter 2:18)

Lure: something or someone tempting or attracting, an appeal or attraction, a decoy. Used in catching animals, especially artificial bait used for catching fish. To attract by *wiles*.

Decoy: A means used to trap, mislead or lure into danger, to lure into danger or trap by or as if by ensnarement.

Entice: to beguile by arising false hope or desire, to lure, to instigate. (*See* Gen. 22:16; Deut. 13:6; Judges 14:15; 16:5; II Chron. 18:19-21; Prov. 1:10; Job 31:27; Jer. 20:10.)

Wiles: a deceitful stratagem or trick intended to ensnare or deceive; also a beguiling or playful trick. (*See* Num. 25:18; Eph. 6:11.)

Seduce: to draw one away from duty or proper conduct (I Cor.15:33); corrupt, to *induce* to have sexual intercourse, to beguile or entice into a desired position or state, to win over, attract. (*See* Mark 13:22; Rev. 2:20; II Kings 21:9.)

Beguile: to mislead by deception: cheat; to distract the attention of: divert; to charm: delight. (*See* Genesis 3:13; Num. 25:18; Col. 2:4; II Peter 2:14.)

Satan uses temptations to inject poison into our being, — spirit, soul and body. He attempts to thwart the functionality of our organs and component parts of our being. Satan does all he can to disable us from performing righteous, holy acts and to enable us to perform unrighteous, sinful acts. The quickened human spirit, made alive by the Holy Spirit, is recreated to commune with God, receive revelatory knowledge from God and receive guidance from the Holy Spirit. Satan, through temptations, attempts to hinder, then halt, our communion and fellowship with God. When satan cuts off our revelatory knowledge flowing from communion with God, he easily deceives us into believing our directions are coming from God, when in fact, they are coming from him! Once satan infiltrates the human spirit, he then attacks the soul. The human soul is renewed for the purposes of possessing the mind of Christ (Phil.2:5), placing our affections on things above, not on the earth (Col. 3:2), and finally, choosing to say "yes" to the will of God. The human soul is the steward of the human spirit, carrying out its orders in partnership with the Holy Spirit. By disabling the functionality of the human soul, God's power is stifled or choked within us. Without God's power freely flowing to renew us, we possess a carnal mind, desiring earthly, corruptible things and we choose our will (in collusion with satan's will) over God's will. When the human soul malfunctions, the body follows suit. The human body is the external instrument of expression through which we express God's love and compassion to serve the saved and evangelize the unsaved. Our senses, which are located in our bodies, allow us to receive and feel other human needs, and the senses are used to assist in meeting those needs. By immobilizing our bodies, the work of the ministry is delayed, souls continue to die without the knowledge of Jesus Christ and many never experience the love and grace of God. Satan is on a mission to defeat and destroy the cause of Christ in every believer. He knows what he must do to infiltrate our camps and take our spoils in order to advance his kingdom of darkness.

In every temptation, we find four component parts consistent throughout Scripture, and they are:

1) The Tempter/Temptress—satan, people, places, things and events used to initiate the attempt.

2) The Tempted—every man, woman, boy or girl who is targeted by the tempter to cause to fall in a temptation.

3) The Temptation—conditions, circumstances, environment, influences, events, states: mental, emotional, spiritual, volitional. The stage, the scenes and the props designed to cause the tempted to fall, to cause the attempt to be successful and to cause the tempter to be victorious.

4) The Attempt—the act itself; the attack, the encounter or confrontation of the tempter in the temptation to subdue the will of the tempted.

If we take a close look in the Scriptures at the temptations of Adam and Christ, we will find the four component parts in the temptations of the two federal heads of the old creation and the new creation.

In Adam's temptation, note the following:

1) The Tempter: The serpent
2) The Tempted: Adam and Eve
3) The Temptation: A conversation about eating fruit from the tree of the knowledge of good and evil, located in the Garden of Eden.

4) The Attempt: The serpent wanted to place in, then stir up and appeal to Adam and Eve's desires (lust of the eyes, lust of the flesh and the pride of life). The serpent enticed them to partake of the forbidden fruit, prohibited by the law of God, suggesting that by doing so, they might be as gods themselves, or as wise as God. The serpent knew their yielding to his attempt would cause Adam and Eve to suffer the same fate as his own – eternal separation from God!

In Christ's temptation, note the following:

1) The Tempter: The devil/satan himself
2) The Tempted: Christ
3) The Temptation: Conversations about surrendering to the voice of satan in the wilderness, on a high mountain and in Jerusalem.
4) The Attempt: After Christ had fasted for forty days and nights, satan tried three times to appeal to Jesus to cause Him to submit to his authority. Satan appealed to Jesus' spirit (worship me), soul (presumptuous confidence of His Father's protection) and body (turn stones into bread, fleshly appetites).

The temptations of Adam and Christ are common to all believers because satan's goal is to remove us from the will of God. This book will focus on the eight deadly steps found in temptations. While satan attempts to put a new face on his tricks, his slithering track record dates back to Adam and Eve, and his modus operandi has NOT changed one bit!! We must be prepared to challenge temptation by knowing the plot of the enemy, and more importantly, knowing that satan will flee from Spirit controlled believers. "Submit yourselves therefore to God. Resist the devil, and he will flee from you" (James 4:7). We can be victorious through Christ if we follow in His steps. When the devil dared Jesus to cast Himself down from the temple's pinnacle, *satan* said "For it is written, He [God] shall give His angels charge over Thee, to keep Thee: And in their hands, they shall bear Thee up, lest at any time Thou shall dash Thy foot against a stone" (Luke 4:10-11). Satan quoted the Scriptures, yet *misquoted* the Scriptures. He knows them well, and well enough to twist, dilute and deceive all believers, from the babe in Christ, to the mature Bible scholar! Jesus defeated the devil as He personified and embodied the Word of God and declared "It is said, Thou shalt not tempt the Lord thy God (Luke 4:12). What did the devil do? "...he departed from Him for a season" (Luke 4:13). Believers, we too must find consistency in the Scriptures to help us to comprehend and respond to each deadly step common to satan's temptations against mankind.

"But every man is tempted when he is drawn away of his own lust and enticed. Then when lust hath conceived, it bringeth forth sin; and sin, when it is finished, bringeth forth death" (James 1:14,15). The inspiration of God given to James magnifies before our eyes the eight deadly steps found in a temptation. The revelation is absolutely enlightening! He discloses through use of the word "drawn", that falling into temptations is a step-by-step process, whether gradual or fast, its process is methodical and deliberate. To be "drawn" suggests that the temptation cycle is well thought out, planned and plotted. Satan, the mischievous one, is the author of such trickery and treachery. He attempts to draw us away from God to himself through whatever means possible, whereas God draws us to

Himself, away from satan, sin, self and the lusts of the world, through his loving kindness (Jer. 31:3).

No matter what we think or say, every temptation of the enemy is directed against the "inner man". No matter what we ascribe to or confess, every temptation is comprised of steps that lead to the rise and fall of every believer. These steps are consistent throughout Scripture and personal testimonies. "There is no temptation but such as is common to man..." (I Cor. 10:13), revealing to us that in every temptation, there are sequential, identifiable steps that are taken by every believer before he or she is bound and separated from God. By the power of the Holy Spirit, we are attempting to take in snapshot forms, slide by slide, a detailed look at temptation's cycle. This event can take place in milliseconds in the hearts and minds of believers! By slowing down the process and examining it closely, we believe that we can disturb, disrupt and destroy not only the flow, but also the integral workings of the enemy against our "inner man". By exposing satan's strategies, believers become better equipped and more determined than ever to render him inoperative. When satan's tactics are exposed and rebuked, we are free to enjoy the many benefits of Christ reigning victoriously in our lives. Let's take a closer look at the eight deadly steps involved in every temptation!

INTERNAL STRUGGLES CONCEALED

Chapter Two
Step 1: The Stimulation of the Senses

The first step common to every temptation is the *stimulation of the senses.* We receive and process information through these physical receptors that enable us to touch, see, smell, taste and hear. Satan always makes his move to arouse, titillate and excite us through these familiar portals. In fact, the enemy's first knock on the door of our senses is the most critical step in a temptation, because no battle is ever won without an initial attack! Believers, beware of satan's subtle gestures! Since the moment of conception, before the first kick in the womb, our senses have been exposed to a constant bombardment of stimuli. Overlooking or improperly filtering what we see, taste, touch, smell or hear can result in a fall from the grace of God. The unsuspecting believer is the prime target of satan, who seeks to destroy us before we even realize we've been hit. "Be sober, be vigilant; because your adversary the devil, as a roaring lion, walketh about, seeking whom he may devour" (I Peter 5:8). There is wisdom in knowing the approach of the enemy. Satan's advance to tempt the believer can enter the senses as smoothly as a stealth bomber flies into forbidden airspace. By design, stealth technology goes virtually undetected by radar, so the element of surprise allows no time to prepare a formidable defense from the enemy. Satan operates in much the same way, without regard for "no fly zone" rules. He invades our senses in an attempt to quickly penetrate our minds. Believers too often make the mistake of assuming that temptation begins in the mind or heart, so we are distracted looking the other way when information enters into our being through the open doors of our senses. Oh, the cunning craftiness of the enemy to cover up his schemes! Beware of satan's deceptive approach!

"But every man is tempted when he is drawn away..." (James 1:14). Man is initially drawn away or drawn out of the Spirit through outside activities or influences, which stimulate the senses. Temptation starts a process in motion *away* from the Spirit of God! If we dissect the word "away", we find two syllables, i.e., *a* and *way*. The first, "a" is often used as a prefix in Greek, Latin and English to negate, meaning "un" or "not". The second syllable, "way", is synonymous with Christ in the Gospel of John. "Jesus saith unto him [doubting Thomas], I am the way..." (John 14:6). When we examine "away" under this narrow scope, we find quite an offensive four letter word! Let's take another look at the text, "...every man is tempted when he is drawn away...". Can you see it? We are subject to fall to temptation when we are "*not* in Christ"! The tempter does not want us abiding in, talking in and walking in Jesus. Therefore, satan, as cleverly as possible, attempts to lead the believer down a path to temporary or total destruction and separation from God.

Satan's initial approach towards man is a "one-two-punch" on our senses. He first attempts to desensitize us from God and His purpose for our lives. If the first blow succeeds, then he strikes the second blow by sensitizing us to his destructive purposes on earth. Satan begins the process by hardening our hearts through our senses. "For the law of the Spirit of life in Christ Jesus hath made me free from the law of sin and death" (Rom. 8:2). In this passage of Scripture, Paul is inspired by God to reveal two opposing laws—one the law of the Spirit of life in Christ Jesus, and the other the law of sin and death. When believers abide in Christ, the Spirit gives life to the new man and releases us from the shackles of our fleshly old man. When satan desensitizes us from God, he causes us to grieve and quench the Spirit. We are left defenseless and hopelessly bound by sin. Temptation flows in a vicious cycle that can spin out of control the instant we allow satan to infiltrate our senses. Shhhhhhh.... Listen. Can you hear it? Can you feel it? Can you taste, smell or see it? The consequences of overlooking the enemy's attack on the senses can kill our fellowship with God. Be alert! Satan will take advantage of the slightest opening or opportunity to destroy the human spirit and harden our hearts. In rapid fire succession, he will alter our minds, numb our emotions and debilitate our wills. Once the will is weakened, the body is soon demoralized, and the law of sin and death has run its course. Make no mistake about it! Satan's will concerning all believers is to pave a smooth and deliberate path to death and destruction. His tactics are never honorable because satan seeks to take over man's entire being (spirit, soul and body) as his mistress, steward and servant for the fulfillment of his own diabolical, selfish will.

We liken the enemy's stimulation of our senses to the sounding of the whistle before the train starts to move down the tracks.... the boarding of the passengers on a flight to a destination called "nowhere"!.... or the soothing voice of the pilot welcoming aboard his passengers as the plane taxis down the runway. The enemy's knock can tickle our ears and whet our appetites. Satan's appeal to our senses is as tempting and predictable as the heat before the passion. Oh, indeed the wiles of the devil are familiar, and leave little doubt about what should follow. We *expect* the singing of the National Anthem before the game, the ringing of the bell before the opening round of a championship bout or the turning of the key in the ignition before cranking up the engine. We are all too familiar with the spark before the fire, the calm before the storm or the stretch before the activity, yet we are most unfamiliar with the initial attack of the enemy. Something is wrong with that picture! When satan makes his first move to get our attention, he is raring to go—on his mark, ready to come out of the starting blocks with great anticipation to complete his goal of undermining the person and work of the believer.

What is so special about the senses? Why would satan make them his first stop? "The pleasure principle." Through the faculties of sensation, man experiences physical gratification and pleasure. We receive and process knowledge and information through sight, sound, taste, touch and smell. By captivating our senses, satan initially gains access to the body of man. How? Logistics. Senses are located in our bodies, attached to our emotions, and connect us to the world, i.e., the world system, people and things of the world. Through these portals, satan gains entry to our mind, will and emotions (the soul of man). He then programs our thinking, feeling and choosing, and this cycle repeats throughout our life span prior to our acceptance of Christ. Can you imagine that? All of our natural lives, satan has been programming into our minds, wills and emotions information that would conform us to his image and character. He has been tailoring our social, political, mental, emotional and habitual predilections from day one. The way we walk, talk, dress, eat, mate and date are no exclusions. All of our choices, from the cars we drive, to the homes we buy, our perspectives for the future, the way we interact with one another, our prejudices, our opinions, etc., have been affected and impacted by satan. He utilizes our senses as input devices. Satan feeds us secret, subtle and sinister data. Being the master deceiver that he is, satan can camouflage his damaging acts in a fog of good deeds. He tries to overload our senses with infected data to cause our systems to freeze up and crash. When all else fails on the personal computer, a last resort keyboard combination is "control, alt, delete". Simultaneously pressing the "Ctrl", "Alt" and "Delete" keys twice on the keyboard constitutes an improper shutdown. A forced termination of the system offers no guarantees that the computer will reboot in exactly the same condition before the fault. Satan works our senses the way a hacker works a p.c. He intentionally violates believers to overload the senses. Watch this! When we yield to the tempter's attack, improperly shut down, collect ourselves, "reboot" or come back up, we are damaged goods because satan has control of us! He has altered our mindset by deleting the Word of God from the hard drives of our soul. Satan has rebooted our systems with his operating system and his corrupt applications. We are rendered totally inept to do the will of God. Instead of being able to apply agape love to a brother or sister in need, we now supply conditional, questionable love. Instead of being non-judgmental when a believer falls, we become super critical. Instead of praying for someone who is going through, we backbite and gossip about their issues. When we allow the enemy access to our "inner man", we usher in hazardous, self-righteous manifestations of satan's influence.

Our senses are similar to motion detection devices. They absorb all movement and activity around us, much like motion sensors in our houses, on our windows and lodged near our doors. When these motion detectors are operating properly, they notify us of any predetermined movement or activity. When our senses are operating properly under the control of God, they have the predetermined ability to detect the presence of evil, and signal to our renewed minds a breach of security in the house. Satan attempts to reprogram our alarm systems by breaking and changing the access code to digits only he and his imps will recognize. When the powers of darkness monitor our house, the carnal mind will sound an alarm at the slightest movement from God or His Word to signal a "breaking and entering" into our comfort zones. Remember, satan's plan is to work his plan to separate us from God unto himself. "For when we were in the flesh, the motions of sins, which were by the law, did work in our members to bring forth fruit [an inward attitude and an outward action] unto death" (Rom. 7:5). This passage speaks volumes on how satan, working through the law, activated our motion sensors, created a commotion within our emotions, gained access to our houses (souls), resurrected our flesh, employed our members (hands, feet, mouth, etc.) and injected spiritual death (separation from God) into our spirits. This is why it is so important to recognize, step by step, how satan operates in a temptation!

Our senses are input devices which introduce data into our minds, and this information is used for responding to life. We eat the foods we eat or sometimes overeat (sweets, fruits, steaks, fries, chips, candy, chicken, shrimp, bread, yogurt) because we have been programmed to like them. We watch the television programs we watch or become addicted to (Oprah, Jerry Springer, The West Wing, HBO, soaps, news, documentaries, cartoons) because we have been programmed to enjoy them. We desire the women or men we lust after (tall or short, thin or full figured, long or short hair, urban or rural, white or blue collar) because we have been programmed to desire them. We enjoy fragrances (expensive perfumes, favorite colognes and the aromas of certain foods, e.g., freshly baked apple pie) because we are programmed to appreciate them. Satan programs us to desire particular people, places, things and events, and then uses them against us to entrap and ensnare us in his vicious web of tricks and treats. We should never lose sight of the fact that satan has been programming us all of our lives through our senses, and we don't even realize it!

Through our five senses, we become world-conscious. There is an institutional relationship between the body's senses and our minds. What we see, hear, smell, taste and touch have a great influence on instructing our minds to move the body into action. Think of the senses as "tenured professors" or instructors in the body, and the body as the "university of the brain". Who is the "president" of the body? Satan, the tempter, is running his program through our senses to control our minds and bodies! He dictates the course material and the degrees offered. The material presented to and taught by our professors (the senses), comes from the president (satan). This material becomes the sensory knowledge programmed into our minds on a daily basis. This information stored in our brains flows from the world system. The world system's approach and responses to life's circumstances is contrary to God's Word. "For all that is in the world, the lust of the flesh, and the lust of the eyes, and the pride of life, is not of the Father, but is of the world" (I John 2:16). Satan programs our views on education, science, politics, marriage, sex, music, etc. through this world system (*kosmos* in the Greek). The world system is called "wicked" in I John 5:19 and is under the temporary control of satan, "the god of this world" (II Cor. 4:4). Sensory knowledge is the knowledge possessed by the natural man or the man who only possesses the Adamic nature. The natural man is a fleshly, sense-oriented man under the control and dominion of satan. That is why the Bible teaches us that "the natural man receiveth not the things of the Spirit of God: for they are foolishness unto him" (I Cor. 2:14). Sensory knowledge can be activated by the carnal man, who possesses both the Adamic and Divine natures. The "spirit of the world" (I Cor. 2:12) attempts to attach itself to us, through our senses, in order to distract us from that which pertains to God. This adverse spirit makes us vulnerable to the things of the world, and causes us to think we are without the power to overcome the things of this world. Thank God that we know satan is a liar, and that we possess within us the Divine nature and life to overcome him and his tricks! Hallelujah!

Let's revisit the events in the Garden of Eden, where the first temptation is introduced. The subtle serpent approaches Eve, and speaks to her sense of hearing. Notice the conversation between Eve and the serpent. In Genesis 3:1, the serpent spoke to the woman contrary to God's commandment. The serpent began his approach to distract her from the truth. He not only stimulated her sense of hearing, but also stimulated her sense of sight to desire the goodness of the forbidden fruit. Listen to the subtlety and craftiness of the serpent speaking to Eve. "For God doth know that in the day ye eat thereof, then your eyes shall be opened, and ye shall be as gods, knowing good and evil" (Gen. 3:5). Her eyes would be opened alright! This first sin opened the eyes of an entire human race. Next, the serpent appealed to Eve's sense of touch as she took the fruit. Finally, the fall was committed when she tasted the fruit. The only sense that was not in total operation was the sense of smell. She could not, figuratively speaking, smell the danger that lurked before her. However, she was quite nosey, probing into God's business! Eve's disobedience made us all subject to the enemy's embattlement of stimulating our senses, capturing our minds, wills and emotions, leading to the enslavement of our bodies. This one commission of sin separated the human spirit from God, and the vicious cycle of temptation was flung into motion. Oh, Sister Eve! What a fatal, costly mistake!

The sin of Adam and Eve passed down through the generations upon the human race. Do you remember the sin of Achan? After the battle of Jericho, the land was left in ruins. With the exception of one family, God cursed Jericho and everything in it. God commanded Joshua and the children of Israel to leave the spoils of Jericho untouched, or they too would be cursed (Joshua 6:18). Achan was of the tribe of Judah, subject to God's commandment, but he was tempted, and got "caught up" by what he saw. Listen to his confession to Joshua. "When I saw among the spoils a goodly Babylonish garment, and two hundred shekels of silver, and a wedge of gold of fifty shekels weight, then I coveted them, and took them; and behold, they are hid in the earth in the midst of my tent, and the silver under it" (Joshua 7:21). True to form, satan first attacked Achan through his senses. He first saw the spoils, coveted them, took them and then hid them under his tent. When Achan disobeyed God, he separated himself and all of the house of Israel from God. Under the law, Achan was stoned to death for his sin. His fate was sealed because his senses were out of control.

In II Samuel 11, the tragic story of King David's sin of covetousness, adultery and murder is revealed. King David knew the law, and he knew that Bathesheba was married, yet his fall into temptation was real. Satan tempted King David through his senses. David first saw Bathsheba from the rooftop, and coveted her, and then he took her and made love to her, awakening his sense of touch. You know the rest of the story—David placed Bathsheba's husband in harm's way on the front line of battle so that he would be killed. Man's elevated positions on earth are satan's folly. Even a king is vulnerable to temptation because satan programs certain appetites and desires into all flesh, making it weak and subject to him (I Cor. 10:12). No one is an exception to the rule!

Samson is another Bible character who fell to temptation. When he visited a place called Timnath, he saw a woman of the daughters of the Philistines. Samson liked what he saw, and rather forcefully asked his parents "now therefore get her for me to wife" (Judges 14:2). Samson knew that he was to take a wife from among his brethren as they were covenant people, yet he fell when he chose that which appealed to his own lustful eye.

The senses are the entry points used by satan to draw us away from the plan and purposes of God for our lives. Just as he tricked Adam and Eve, satan remains on the job to tempt us to commit sin. He still bombards the senses in an attempt to gain entry to our minds. Believers, remember King David's plight! God has called us to be pastors, preachers, deacons, trustees, singers, and teachers. We might be beautiful or hard working people, yet we must be mindful that satan would be delighted to deceive us into thinking that the constant praises we hear are of our own goodness. Our sense of hearing, albeit natural, is a powerful portal of entry. When we allow the praises of man to infiltrate our ears and "go to our heads" (minds), then we are in grave danger of the emotions and the will tripping the body to take a fall. "Pride goeth before destruction, and an haughty spirit before a fall" (Prov. 16:18).

Remember Achan's fall! Both his sense of sight and touch were out of control. He first saw the spoils of Jericho before he took them against the commandment of God. What a costly price he paid! His disobedience brought damnation to himself, his household and his nation. When we see clothes, jewelry, food, cars, houses, women, men and children that we have no business with, and go full speed ahead to acquire the forbidden, then our sense of sight is out of control. We've all "been there" and "done that". Temptation is satan's weapon to destroy us. He will put that very thing in front of us so that we will fall. We might visit a neighbor's house and see items of interest to us, and if we are not careful, we will find ourselves taking things that do not belong to us, e.g., money or valuables. We see attractive co-workers, and fall prey to temptation in the workplace. If we allow our senses to spin out of control, we can easily open the floodgates to more temptation. Before we know it, the ears hear "oh, you look so good", and the next thing we know, the sense of touch engages and there we are inappropriately falling into the forbidden arms of another weak vessel. Understand that the attack begins through our senses. The senses of smell and taste are no less elusive. Picture this. We're relaxing on the couch, and the aroma of that apple pie overwhelms us. Although the doctor has just told us that all sweets are off limits for our condition, we yield first to our sense of smell, and then we get up and *look* in the kitchen and *see* that pie, and if we're not careful, it's over when we get right down to the "nitty gritty" and somehow justify opening the door to our sense of taste! It's a process—a dangerous one! Yielding to temptation can kill us. "For the wages of sin is death, but the gift of God is eternal life through Jesus Christ our Lord" (Rom. 6:23).

How important it is for us to understand the steps in a temptation! Truly, we perish for the lack of knowledge. Satan does not want us to understand how he operates through our senses. There are demons vexed right now because this book is exposing their game! Hallelujah!! The

Bible teaches us in Romans 13:14, "make not provision for the flesh", and in Ephesians 4:27, "neither give place to the devil". When we give occasion to our senses to be stimulated by satan, we are opening ourselves up to potentially losing our anointing, losing our positions in the church, losing our families, losing our jobs, losing our homes, losing respect and potentially missing out on the blessings of the Kingdom. One wrong glance held too long, one taste of the wrong food, one sniff or snort too many, one careless touch of the forbidden, one stroll down musical memory lane, and there it is—satan has exposed an area of weakness in us for his own gain and future operations. We must not underestimate the work of satan through our senses. He uses these openings to build thoughts, choices and lustful desires into us. This is how he mates the external things of the world with the internal thoughts, choices and lusts in our hearts. We must make every effort to ensure that we understand the tactics and strategies of his operations if we are to experience victory daily in our lives. Now, let us take a look at Step Two in a temptation: Sowing of the Seed in the Mind.

Chapter Three
Step 2: The Sowing of the Seed in the Mind

The second step common to every temptation is the *sowing of the seed in the mind.* James 1:14 teaches us that every man is tempted in his heart or mind and drawn away by his thoughts. The Spirit of God continues to unravel the twisted web that satan has spun to apprehend the believer.

As we learned in Chapter Two, satan begins his attempt on the believer by stimulating or activating one or more of the five senses. The tempter uses our senses as a means to capture or divert our attention from the Lord and the things of His Kingdom. Satan desires to keep us focused on sinful, good, selfish or worldly thoughts. Sinful thoughts are fleshly, blatant and contrary to Scripture. Sinful thoughts precede sinful acts. We know that to steal, lie, cheat, murder, fornicate or commit adultery is to sin. When we sin, we separate ourselves from God (Gal. 5:19-21). Why then would we entertain sinful thoughts? Believers determined to be on the Lord's side must know the tricks of the enemy, and make a careful, prayerful effort to steer clear of sinful thoughts.

There is a new twist, however, when we consider *good* thoughts. Interestingly enough, good thoughts can appear healthy and selfless on the surface, while their underlying purpose, known or unknown, hinders the will of God for our lives. For example, in Matthew 16:21–23, Jesus revealed His fate in Jerusalem to His disciples. Peter chose not to accept the outcome, and began to rebuke Jesus, saying "Be it far from Thee, Lord: this shall not be unto Thee". Jesus knew Peter's thoughts and the condition of his heart, so He turned to him and rebuked satan, ***not*** Peter. Why? Christ recognized

Peter meant well, but was temporarily under the influence of satan. Peter had the right idea, but the wrong spirit in operation. Satan will never cease to deceive the believer. The enemy always attempts to hide behind good thoughts and honorable intentions to trap us into savoring those things which are not of God, but of man or satan. Consider the miracle of Jesus feeding a multitude of five thousand men with five loaves of bread and two small fish (John 6:1-15). After accomplishing so great a feat, the people wanted to make Jesus their earthly king. While the desires of the people were truly honorable, their timing was off. When Jesus perceived that the crowd would forcefully overtake Him to make Him a king, "He departed again into a mountain himself alone" (John 6:15). Jesus had to flee because he perceived once again that the people meant well, but a good thought had run amuck! Had they made Jesus an earthly king, He would have forgone the cross, and we would all still be living, thinking and acting out of uncontrollable flesh. There would be no new birth (regeneration), no new standing before God (righteousness and justification), no power to overcome sin (sanctification) and no new hope for a better future (glorification). Beware of good thoughts that have their origin in self or satan instead of God!

Believers must also watch out for satan's pitfalls that lead to selfish thoughts and deeds. Selfish thoughts are manifest through expressions of self desire, e.g., self-gratification, self-exaltation, self-inflation or self-appreciation. In the Book of Esther, Haman (quite literally) got "hung up" in his own trap of self-importance. The king asked Haman, "What shall be done unto the man the King delighted to honour?" (Esther 6:6) Haman's thoughts are recorded later in that same verse. Being full of himself, Haman suspected the king was pleased with him, so he thought in his heart, "To whom would the King delight to do honour more than myself?" (Esther 6:6) Haman "couldn't see the forest for the trees", or more appropriately, he "couldn't see the truth for thoughts of *self*"! Haman was under the influence of satan, so he could not see that his pride and arrogance were leading him to swift and certain destruction. If we are not careful, we too will find the noose we tie for another wrapped tightly around our own necks (Psalm 7:15,16). Avoid Haman's demise, and be sure your confidence is grounded in the truth of God's Word. "Judgments are prepared for scorners, and stripes for the back of fools" (Prov. 19:29).

In Mark 10:17-22, the rich young ruler knew he had his act together until Jesus exposed the thoughts and intents of his heart. He had a covetous heart, which is a selfish heart with a tight fisted clench. The rich young ruler lost his zeal when Jesus told him to sell all he had and give to the poor in order to gain eternal life. The young man walked away sad because he was more concerned about himself and his wealth than with "treasures in heaven, where neither moth nor rust doth corrupt, and where thieves do not break through nor steal" (Matt. 6: 20).

Worldly thoughts have their origin in satan and the world system, and these thoughts can cause us to become overly concerned with the superficial and material things of this world, such as cars, houses, jewelry, money, position, power, pride, etc. Jesus taught about the dangers associated with a worldly mindset. "And the cares of this world, and the deceitfulness of riches, and the lusts of other things entering in, choke the Word, and it becometh unfruitful" (Mark 4:19).

Godly thoughts originate in God and are purposed to meet spiritual, mental, emotional, physical, social and other vital needs. Jesus said "The Son can do nothing of Himself, but what He seeth the Father do, for what things soever He doeth, these also doeth the Son likewise" (John 5:19). After healing the lame man at the pool of Bethsaida on the Sabbath day, Jesus acknowledged His Sonship or relationship to God, and He stilled the voices and actions of the Jews. Jesus was saying that all of His actions were initiated in thought by the Father and governed by His Spirit. This is why we must follow in the Master's footsteps, and scrutinize the source, origin and underlying purpose of our thoughts.

The mind is the organ of thought that receives and processes information. Through the mind, we are equipped to know, think, imagine, remember and understand. Our intellect, reasoning, wisdom and cleverness all pertain to the mind. Think of the mind as a projection or television screen or computer monitor, where information of interest is received, transmitted and displayed via external and internal sources. Television screens and computer monitors display signals received from outside the home or housed unit. These signals then transmit the data through the electronic machinery sitting on the tv stand or desk inside our homes, and we enjoy our favorite commercials, network programming, cable channels or website. The mind works in very much the same manner. We first receive data from external sources. Remember the senses—the points of entry. Satan transmits temptation through the senses to be processed in our minds as thoughts and desires. We are learning that every temptation is provoked by thought, so it is important for us to seek the mind of God and cling to godly thoughts in order to keep the victory.

Watch out! Through our minds, satan begins his manipulation process to design, devise and orchestrate our fall. He attempts to deceive us by channeling the information we receive in order to change our beliefs. This is why it is so important for us to monitor what we watch, or the entertainment that amuses us. MTV and BET show music videos throughout the day. Adults and children are influenced daily by what we see and hear plastered on the screens of our televisions. Acts of violence, flirtatious and seductive dancing with sexual implications, steamy and degrading lyrics are seen, heard and acted out in many of these videos. Those who feed on this programming are negatively influenced by what they see and hear. Have you ever caught yourself driving down the street or going about your routine in the morning, brushing your hair or shaving, when out of the blue, you hear yourself humming a little tune that catches you off guard? Have you ever wondered "where'd *that* come from?" We have all done it at some point, so we should monitor our programming because what goes in, certainly comes out in one form or another! Believers should be "bringing into captivity every thought to the obedience of Christ" (II Cor.10:5). We must ferociously frisk every thought up and down, so we can detect evil before it enters the doors of our being. Have you ever noticed how some catastrophes happen at schools, clubs, house parties, on the job, etc.? Trouble seems to sniff out a place that lacks security. Without metal detectors, weapons can potentially pass virtually undetected through the doors. What's the problem? The environment is ripe for someone with bad intentions to enter and cause mayhem. If the unthinkable should happen, and someone gets hurt or even killed, then the investigation will beg the questions *Why* or *What* could have been done to prevent this tragedy? If it is found that time was not taken to thoroughly check out the safety of the premises before the event, then some responsible party will have to answer. Someone must pay! The same thing happens to believers. We allow any and every thought to enter our minds, not knowing or caring enough that those thoughts might carry with them sin and death, the twin killers! When they set foot into our minds, they begin to wreak havoc, until they accomplish their two-fold mission to separate and destroy! We cannot afford to sleep on satan because he is definitely not sleeping on us!

Satan's next step is to sow his seeds or thoughts (evil, good, selfish or worldly) into the soil of our minds. If he can plant thoughts in our heads and water them with additional thoughts and desires, then he knows that he will one day see the fruits of his labor – the works of the flesh. The tempter knows according to Genesis 6:5, "that every imagination of the thoughts of the heart are only evil continually"; therefore, if he can sow in the right season and the right cycle, he will reap a great harvest. By swindling us into turning our attention towards him and away from God, satan effectively changes the condition of the heart of the believer from being spiritual to carnal and fleshly. Remember, in order for satan to operate in us, he must shut down our spiritual connection to God! He must cut off the anointing flowing through our spirit from the Holy Spirit. By causing us to operate in the flesh, he hardens our hearts, shuts off the anointing, rendering us unable to receive the Word of God, His power and the understanding that comes from His Word. A hardened heart towards God is a fleshly heart under the control of satan! Conversely, a hardened heart towards satan is a sensitive heart towards God! Therefore, satan must deactivate our connection to God before he can establish a connection with believers. We learned in the previous chapter how satan initially captures the attention of our senses. The deceiver taps his first seed of thought into our beings through the pathways of the eyes, ears, nose, hands or mouth. That is how he consistently sows mind altering thoughts into our being. The enemy attacks with precision to selectively penetrate the portals of our senses to plant seeds of thought to cause our demise. Satan seeks the weakened point of access, the point of vulnerability into our being so he can establish a toehold and bind us up in a stronghold. Stimuli from the senses form what is called "sensory knowledge", which enters the brain for identification, processing and execution. Satan wants us to receive his plan and purposes, identify with and process them in our carnal minds and then execute his thoughts through our fleshly strength and energy. Satan knows that the mind is the central processing unit for transforming data into information for action. The enemy knows that if he can get the mind to process information that does not advance the Kingdom of God, then he has room to move in for himself and his own destructive purposes. Beware! "The thief cometh not, but for to steal, and to kill, and to destroy" (John 10:10).

Satan is a spoiler. He desires to disgrace all believers. He aims to steal our testimony, kill our peace of mind, and most importantly, destroy our fellowship with God. The ultimate goal of satan is to displace godly thoughts from our renewed minds and replace them with his sinister, good or worldly thoughts in our carnal minds. The Bible teaches us in Romans 8:7, that "the carnal mind is enmity [hostile] against God: for it is not subject to the law of God, neither indeed can be". Carnality of mind creates major warfare within the believer against God and His purposes. It rocks and reels against His authority and power. A carnal mind frustrates God's designs for our lives, opposes His interests, salivates in His face and raises objections by arguing and reasoning against God's revelation. Walking under the influence of satan and a carnal mind disturbs the peace of God's Spirit. The battle ensues, introducing a barrage of confusing thoughts. A carnal mind rebels against God's wisdom, by boasting of its own wisdom. A carnal, reprobate mind refuses to submit its will to God's will. Does that describe the mind and desires of satan? Oh, yes indeed! That is precisely his m.o. to the letter! Now, look inward. Are you walking in the Spirit of God or has satan taken hold of your thoughts? Which scenario describes the current condition of your mind? Help us Lord!!

Satan attacks the consciousness of the mind. Satan understands that if he can steer the attention of the mind away from God and in the direction of his exploits, schemes and plots, then he can conform both thoughts and actions of the tempted toward fulfilling his quests. "For as he thinketh in his heart, so is he" (Prov. 23:7). Satan knows the conditions for causing us to fall. If he can trash our thinking capacity with the debris of his thoughts, then it will be only a matter of time before we act out what he has planted into our minds because we *become* our thoughts. Whatever we behold in our thought life, we *behave* accordingly. "For they that are after the flesh do mind the things of the flesh" (Rom. 8:5). The Word of God is clear on this point. They who walk after fleshly appetites, lusts and desires, do so because they have set their minds, structured their environments, established and maintained friendships with fleshly people, places and things.

In a temptation, satan knows how vital it is to arrest the mind of the believer. If he can handcuff the believer's mind, take it into custody, speak to it in order to create doubt about the laws of God, then satan can imprison us within the realm of the flesh and block us from making that one call to our only true advocate, Jesus Christ. He knows that if he apprehends the mind, where attitudes are formed and words and actions are expressed, then he will cause the believer to respond in self and manifest the fleshly, carnal nature. If satan can reshape and reform our attitudes, he can change our behavior.

Satan is on a mission to deceive us. In the Garden of Eden, he deliberately tempted Eve with his smooth appeal "ye shall not surely die" (Gen. 3:4). Eve allowed satan to enter through the portals of her ears, and then penetrate the filters of her mind. It was over when Eve let her carnal, fleshly thoughts rule her actions and understanding of God's instructions.

Do you remember Judas Iscariot? Judas was one of the twelve chosen disciples called by Jesus. Judas walked with Jesus, ate with Jesus, heard Jesus preach and teach, and saw Jesus heal the sick and raise the dead. After ALL of that, he *still* allowed satan to put the thought in his heart to betray Jesus! (John 13:2) By apprehending Judas' mind, satan was able to act out his will in the earth against Jesus.

The following fact bears repeating because it is often ignored or overlooked. If satan can overtake our thoughts, then he can change our behavior to perform sinful habits in our lives. If he can take our focus off the Author and Finisher of our faith, then he knows it will be only a matter of time before we yield to his temptations. The Bible stresses in Romans 12:2 the importance of having our minds renewed in the Word so that our thinking and processing will be transformed into the image of Christ, and not conformed to the world or deformed into the image of satan.

Satan wants the mind of our souls in his temptations so he can resurrect the old self, renew the harbinger of his operations and energize the old man to enjoy the things of the world. When we accept the enemy's thoughts, we begin to feel the old nature coming back to life, desiring fulfillment of the flesh. A surge of power runs through us when we are entertaining satan's thoughts, and it quickens the old man, brings him back to life and allows the body of sin to perform the services of the tempter. In Acts 5:1-11, Ananias and Sapphira both entertained the thoughts of satan. Their carnal thoughts expressed the will of satan, and lied to the Holy Ghost about keeping back a part of the income generated from selling land. Their old natures were resurrected through the words of satan, and they began the thought process in their minds. They conjured up a scheme to overlook their commitment to God. Have you ever broken a promise to God by withholding a portion of your legally earned income? Oh, believers, *beware* of the fall! The Word of God speaks to us: "Will a man rob God? Yet ye have robbed me. But ye say, Wherein have we robbed thee? In tithes and offerings. Ye are cursed with a curse: for ye have robbed me, even this whole nation" (Mal. 3:8,9). Both Ananias and Sapphira lost their lives because of their deception and unwillingness to acknowledge their obligation to God. Satan fulfilled his purpose, which was to steal, kill and destroy their lives (John 10:10). The actions of Ananias and Sapphira also advanced God's purpose, which established His absolute power among all men, women, boys and girls who heard of these events.

Satan can cut off the stream of God's anointed power flowing into our lives by controlling our minds. He plans his work and works his plan to defeat us, and the methods are so tried and tested and sure, that he programs his steps to temptation in much the same way we program the dialing mechanisms on our telephones. Satan attempts to dial up our senses by pressing or stimulating the right numbers. Once he programs the number to our minds, he saves a speed dial to his moves in order to establish faster access for future connections. How does he do it? He stores our numbers in his memory pad and presses the redial feature whenever he needs to engage us for his purposes! This is why it is so dangerous to yield the senses to the enemy.

Watch out for the temptation, and walk in the Spirit to avoid the fall that leads to satan's hard wiring his program within us! Does it matter what we allow our eyes to see? Absolutely! Who cares about what we listen to? God cares, the enemy snares and we must beware! Could a little sniff, touch or taste really do any harm? Most definitely! Believers can fall out of the will of God in an instant by allowing satan free reign. Once the senses are invaded, and the mind is captivated, there is a pattern of defeat lain for future attacks. When we permit the enemy the slightest opening, he is quick to disconnect us from the mind of Christ and habitually endear us to his own agenda. Without the mind of Christ, we are powerless to temptations! Satan's second step in a temptation is dynamic! If he can change the toggle switch of our minds from God to himself, then he can batter us more with his deadly steps in temptation.

Through our minds, satan builds his webs of thought to access the sensory knowledge of all believers. By accessing the mind, he furthers his plan to weaken our will and cause us to fall prey to his temptations. He sows seeds of thought in us that revive the works of the flesh. The fruit always manifests the root. The actions always reveal the state of consciousness. Our actions can always be traced back to the current thoughts running through our minds. "For from within, out of the heart of men, proceed evil thoughts, adulteries, fornications, murders,…" (Mark 7:21). Every evil thought is planted in our hearts and possesses with it an evil corresponding action. Jesus taught us in John 3:6, "That which is born of the flesh is flesh". Evil thoughts do not suddenly change their content and character midstream – once evil in nature, always evil. Jesus also taught in Matthew 7:18, "A good tree cannot bring forth evil fruit, neither can a corrupt tree bring forth good fruit". Before

Eve's act of disobedience to God, she was deceived by lustful, entertaining thoughts from the subtle serpent. Judas' act of betrayal can be traced back to thoughts of betrayal and greed. Cain's act of murder was rooted in thoughts of jealousy, which evolved to rensentful, murderous thoughts. Before Noah cursed Ham for uncovering his nakedness and drunkenness to his brothers, his mind was provoked by thoughts of anger and bitterness.

It is amazing how every action begins with a thought, whether our thoughts, someone else's thoughts, God's thoughts or satan's thoughts. Every thought produces some type of action. When advertisers want us to buy their products, they begin by introducing the product to the delight of our senses. Then they sow appealing seeds into our minds to invoke favorable thoughts about the value of their product and why it surpasses all others. Satan uses the same approach. When he wants us to buy into one of his slick ideas, he exhibits his product (a beautiful woman, a handsome beau, a flashy car, an exotic trip, romantic clothing, mouth watering delicacies, store sales, etc.) before our senses. He then presents the features, advantages and benefits of his product to our minds, hoping we will ignore what God has to offer. Satan then wants us to buy in to his schemes! He can transform himself and his salesmen into angels of light (II Cor. 11:13-15). The tempter is the best false advertiser in and out of this world. The Bible calls satan "the god of this world" (II Cor. 4:4) and "the prince of this world" (John 12:31). As "the prince of the power of the air" (Eph. 2:2), satan uses every imaginable form of media to seduce, incite and deceive the believer into yielding to his temptations. He uses large and small billboards to lure us into buying goods and services that are unhealthy to our spiritual lives. He uses human billboards to parade around before our eyes and sow into our minds desires to have the latest, veneer fashion clothing or to have the person wearing the apparel. He uses human billboards to promote perfumes that arouse our sense of smell. Satan revels in programming our minds with appetizing, sinful thoughts. He uses the radio to stir up our fleshly desires by blaring "oldies but goodies" and activities that fail to give God the glory. He uses the e-mail system to start chain letters attempting to sow fear and confusion into the hearts of individuals. The enemy advertises his messages on moving vehicles, i.e., buses, cars, trains, 18 wheelers and airplanes. He uses books and magazines to spread his gossip, to get us to buy in to his cheap, dishonest rumors about people, places and things. Remember, satan has *no* scruples. He wouldn't think twice about attempting to sell us a bag of sand out on the beach. Satan would sit back, relax and get a kick out of tempting us to buy a block of ice from Antarctica or a chip of paint from the Golden Gate Bridge. Oh, it might sound foolish, but satan's scale goes from the sublime to the ridiculous! He will do whatever it takes to trip up the walk of a believer. The deceiver delights in throwing us off course so we will lose fellowship with God. He could care less about our opportunity in Christ because his primary goal is to cause us to miss the mark and to abort our purpose and destiny for eternal life.

Ananias and Sapphira bought into satan's lies, and it cost them their lives. Abraham and Sarai also fell to the tempter (Gen. 12:11-20). Abraham was sternly rebuked for his transgression, which cost Pharaoh and his house greatly. Isaac and Rebekah allowed satan to sow into their minds thoughts of favoritism towards Esau and Jacob, which created constant, long-term conflict between them (Gen. 25:27-34; 27). Jacob got a taste of his own deceptive medicine when Laban allowed the enemy to plant trickery in his heart (Gen. 29). Jacob manifested thoughts of hatred towards Leah, and those thoughts were planted in his heart by satan (Gen. 29:30-31). Satan sowed jealousy into the heart of Rachel against her sister Leah, because Leah was fertile and she was barren (Gen. 29:31; 30:1). In Genesis 37, Jacob's sons bought into satan's notion to express hatred towards Joseph. In II Samuel 11, David's adulteress, murdering affair began with the senses, creating lustful thoughts in his mind, leading to sinful behavior. Absalom's rebellion and conspiracy against his father, David, was initiated and instigated by satanic thoughts, but accomplished by his own fleshly plotting and scheming (II Sam. 15). In II Chronicles 10, Rehoboam's poor decision to accept counsel from his peers rather than the elders started with a thought, cost him part of the Kingdom, and ended with the life of Hadoram.

Initially, satan sows his seeds of thought, and then he waters them to bring forth corruptible fruit. He programs our carnal fleshly minds with sensory knowledge and then presses the memory recall button to remind us of the existing thought with its desires and purpose. When we repeatedly fail to focus our thoughts on God, the condition of the mind can fully deteriorate or be given over to a reprobate mind (Rom. 1:28), a fleshly mind (Col. 2:18) or a defiled mind (Titus 1:15).

If satan is successful in capturing the believer's thought life, then he moves on to Step Three, which is to "Start the Imagination"!!

Chapter Four
Step 3: Starting the Creativity of the Imagination

The third step common to temptation is *starting the creativity of the imagination*. Now, we see satan's plot thicken. Step by step, he carves a deeper gash into the resolve of the believer with his temptation cycle. If we must be confronted, isn't it good to know the tactics of the enemy, and to know that we have the means (via the Holy Spirit) to totally disarm satan? We are exposing and examining the steps to his plot, so we will know the fundamental elements of temptation. We should expect to be targeted daily. However, if we know his moves and each component of the enemy's arsenal, then we can use this tactical advantage to counter his shots and stand victorious through the battle. Having read this far, have you found yourself memorizing the first few steps of the deceiver's attack? Have you been able to apply this text to your life? If so, that is outstanding news, because you are preparing for a great testimony about giving God the glory in the midst of your spiritual warfare storm! Let's review. What does satan do first? He stimulates our senses. What's his next move? He sows seeds of thought into our minds. Does he stop there? No, indeed! Once he penetrates the senses and gains entry into the mind, he engages another demon to attack with his next blow, *starting the creativity of the imagination*! The imagination is the creative function of the mind, which develops, designs and enhances our thoughts, desires and lusts. Think of the imagination as a booster of the mind, given to add imagery, color and detail to thoughts and ideas. The imagination adds seasonings to our meats, colors to our clothing, personality to our behavior, decorations to our houses, tenaciousness to our dreams, beauty to our ashes, customization to our cars, fertilization to the field of our visions, expectation to our hopes, style to our hairdos, methods to increase our finances, glamour and glitz to our lifestyles, shapes and sizes to our mates and quality to our relationships. The imagination adds an abundance of flare to our thought process. Let's take a closer look at the imagination.

The imagination can be used for good and evil. Initially, Adam used his creative imagination in a godly, powerful way when he named all the animals in the kingdom (Gen. 2:19,20). However, once satan tainted the imagery of Eve's imagination, the function that worked for good, began to operate for evil (Gen. 3:1-7). From that day forward, God recognized the flaw, and said "every imagination of the thoughts of his heart was evil continually" (Gen. 6:5). The Hebrew word for imagination, *yetser* {yay'-tser}, stresses that the imagination and its thoughts and purposes are evil. According to Genesis 8:21, "the imagination of man's heart is evil from his youth". This teaches us that the imagination from a very early stage in life, is under the sinful, creative energy of satan. In Genesis 11:6, the Lord stated that the imagination has the power to bring to pass without restraint that which it has conceived. Look at that! Read it again! That's the power of the imagination, and we did not say it, but the Word of God said it! That is why so many times when those murderous, violent, suicidal, sinful, hurtful, revengeful, unforgiving, hateful, bitter, resentful, deceitful, envious, covetous, adulteress thoughts enter into our minds, they have such a control over our attitudes and actions. The imagination takes those thoughts, develops and designs the entire scenario, attaches its two cents worth, and then runs rampant with it.

We have an overwhelming tendency to encourage use of the imagination, without recognizing its power when yielded to the wrong source. We must know and always acknowledge that the imagination can be more harmful than helpful. Why do you think that when satan sends a thought to our mind, he immediately attempts to activate the creative power of the imagination? If he can take a thought and dress it up and make it look good enough to us, then it will be only a matter of time before we lose total focus of God to concentrate on the imagery of the thought and yield to its desires. After satan opened up Eve's senses, and planted a thought in her mind, he immediately caused her imagination to kick in, which resulted in her lusting after the fruit from the tree, and the rest is history. He does the same thing to us! He stimulates our senses, sows a thought into our mind, and then starts in operation the creative juices of the imagination. Men look at women and begin to undress them with their imagination. Women lust after men and start desiring them and envisioning them in immoral ways. Married individuals crave for the untouchable through the power of the imagination. People begin to covet the possessions of another when the imagination gets out of hand. Murders take place because someone watching television or a movie does not realize that satan is sowing the deed in seed form, a thought.

Satan delights in encouraging the imagination to visualize sin, and achieve it. Thieves imagine robbing banks before they attempt the heist. Hustlers first imagine getting rich, owning houses, cars and jewelry, and then they set out to realize their grandiose thoughts, no matter how short lived the thrill might be. Business men and women launder money and believe they can get away with it because the imagination made them think they could accomplish it. Children and young people imagine making it big as rappers and singers, only to get trapped in the world of make believe or "Hollywood". The imaginations of Hollywood's producers, directors and script writers have taken sex, violence, and virtual reality movies to another level. Hollywood has been infiltrating the souls of man, planting future acts of murder, violence, deception, betrayal, lying and fear into the hearts of men and women, boys and girls everywhere. As we are writing now, one of the major networks is broadcasting a movie which highlights a serial killer who preys on virgin males and females. The current scene features a "pop your cherry" party, where young people can lose their virginity in order to avoid the killer's attack. What is wrong with this picture? How sexually explicit must movies get? How tainted are the imaginations of the writers! How violent is too violent? When do we pull the plug on these movies and realize the imagination has overstepped its boundaries? How many ways can we find to kill someone, hang someone, cut up someone, blast someone, and decapitate someone, before we understand the damage of the imagination under satan's control?

Satan delights in overloading the imagination circuits of all believers. The tempter stirs up our internal lusts with external desires, hoping to create a spontaneous combustion! Satan is busy using movies, television, books and any other media or mechanism to stimulate our imaginations into believing a fantasy. Is there an escape? Oh yes! We can defeat the tempter's ploy by maintaining the mind of Christ. Before satan influences twist the imagination's ungodly dreams into sinful reality, rebuke him in the name of Jesus!!

Satan knows that an overactive imagination can lead to separation from the Kingdom of God. In fact, he has first-hand knowledge. Don't you remember? Satan, himself, fell prey to his own imagination, and his illusions of grandeur resulted in his fall from heaven (Isaiah 14:12-15). Lucifer (satan) was in trouble the moment he imagined he would be like God. Satan spoke his own pathway to destruction! Examine what he said and how quickly his demise followed the utterance of the five "I wills" in the imagination of his heart, "I will ascend into heaven; I will exalt my throne above the stars of God; I will sit also upon the mount of the congregation, in the sides of the north; I will ascend above the heights of the clouds; I will be like the most High". The power or influence of the imagination can cause believers to lose total sight of their appointed and anointed roles, their God given responsibility, their known accountability and their revealed purpose. This is exactly what happened to satan, and the crisis exists in the lives of many believers within the church today. How often do we enjoy and witness God's favor, only to be confounded by the trip that so awkwardly precedes the fall?

We learned earlier in Chapters Two and Three that the process of the fall begins with the enemy's knock on the portals of our senses. Somebody listens to a vile word, sniffs or tastes the forbidden, sees or even touches the trap. The trap does exactly what traps are designed to do. It *bites* and gains entry to the mind through the opening. We are now learning the danger of the imagination when thoughts are entertained and whipped up in the mind to the point of distortion. Under satan's influence, the imagination gets *caught up*, and then the fall ensues. The process can be compulsive and seem to occur in an instant or it can be a work in progress over a span of minutes, days, weeks, months or years.

Know the enemy's press on our imaginations. He has no barriers. His mission is accomplished by our fall, and he has no respect of persons or places. Our homes, communities, workplaces and churches are only a few of his favorite targets of sport. Oh yes! Satan's "got game", and he seeks to play the imaginations of every believer each moment of every day! Believers are only pawns in satan's game when we choose to play on his team. Are you being pawned by the enemy in your imagination while sitting among the faithful few? Surely you know satan goes to church. He's in the house early, and looks specifically for YOU! Can you relate to the enemy's sport with the imagination in the following scenarios?

- The imagination envisions that you will be the pastor of your church, because in your mind, you believe that you preach and/or teach better than your pastor.
- In your imagination, you are sure that men, women, boys and girls should bow down to you, worship and adore you because you have a talented singing voice.
- In your imagination, you are convinced that since the church is without the pastor, that you will assume all pastoral functions and duties, and run the church.
- In your imagination, because you pay your tithes and have been doing so for many years, you should have your own pew and the final "say so" in any matter pertaining to church business.

If you can relate to any of the above, then you are familiar with satan's moves against the members of the Body of Christ. No matter how out of control people and circumstances might seem, the Word of God remains unscathed. There *is* a way of escape. "There hath no temptation taken you but such as is common to man: but God is faithful, who will not suffer you to be tempted above that ye are able; but will with the temptation also make a way to escape, that ye may be able to bear it" (I Cor. 10:13).

Temptation and satan's influence on the imagination not only go to church, but also swing full tilt in our secular lives. On the job, our imagination tricks us into believing that we are the best employee or thing to happen to the industry since "sliced bread". We become full of *self*, and imagine we should receive all the bonuses, obtain all of the letters of appreciation and commendation, earn all of the compensatory time and secure every promotion. In our homes, we are convinced that we are the best spouse or mate, boyfriend or girlfriend, friend or acquaintance, cook or cleaner, conversationalist or activist, parent or child, lover or forgiver. We are persuaded in our own imaginations that we drive the fanciest cars, live in the most plush homes, possess the most diversified portfolios, travel to the most exotic cities, cruise the finest ocean liners or work for the greatest Fortune 500 companies. We think we've got it going on above any other because we are employed by the government for more than twenty or thirty years, dine at the classiest restaurants, fly first class only, entertain and socialize among the "who's who" elite, etc. As we can see, when the imagination is alienated from the life of God, it deceives us into believing that we are more than we truly are. The danger exists in believing we are "all that"!

In Acts 12:21-23, upon a set day, King Herod, who thought he was God, died. Why? Because one day he stood up to make a speech, and the people in their own imaginations, revered him as a god, and he accepted the praise as if he were God. He drank from the cup of death and damnation when he failed to give the glory to the one and only true God. Satan programmed Herod's imagination into thinking that he was a god. By the same code, satan programmed the imaginations of the people into seeing Herod as a god, and heralding him as if he were a god. Herod's inward pride, coupled with the people's outward praise for him, created a spontaneous combustion, which resulted in the fall and physical destruction of this man. Herod's demise was similar to what happened to satan. Although satan has not died physically as Herod, he did fall, and soon and *very* soon, he will be separated from us for all eternity, Hallelujah! Because pride can be formed in the heart through the power of the imagination (Luke 1:51), we must "cast down imaginations and every high thing that exalteth itself against the knowledge of God" (II. Cor. 10:5). The imagination puffs up the flesh, while deflating the spirit. The imagination of man forms images in the mind, which can become icons in the life of the individual, which can become little gods, which cause us to worship and serve them. They conform us to their purposes, which result in breaking the commandments of God, "thou shalt have no other gods before me..., thou shalt not make unto thee any graven images..., thou shalt not bow down thyself to them, nor serve them" (Exodus 20:3-5). This is why Jehovah of the Old Testament was so adamant, so unbending with the Children of Israel about cutting down (Lev. 26:30), breaking down (Exodus 23:24), destroying (Num. 33:52) and burning the graven (Deut. 7:5), molten (Num. 33:52) and carved (II Chron. 34:3,4) images in their lives and in the lives and land of their enemies. He warned them not to become ensnared with their images (Deut. 12:30), because those idols would turn their hearts from Him, and reproduce such desires within their souls and their seed (Deut. 7:4). The commandment was unrelenting. Jehovah knew that given a little bit of rope, the Children of Israel would tie their own noose by rejecting Him, the only true God, and worshipping, serving and sacrificing unto false gods (II Kings 17:15-17).

The imagination's goal under the control of satan and the flesh is to cause the believer to commit idolatry, that is, to worship and serve him, and denounce and reject God. Satan wants us to serve the gold, silver, brass and human idols of the world. He uses idols to tempt and trap us into worshipping and serving him. Idols such as people, power, pleasure, passion, praise, popularity and provision. When is the last time you became so mesmerized by a man, woman, boy or girl, that you nearly or completely lost your capacity to make godly decisions involving that person? Don't be deceived by the world's living, breathing portraits of smoke and mirrored love, lust and loyalty. Satan paints and taints our imaginations, and then presents human images to us for the sole purpose of separating us from the love of God. The person giving you the fit in your life might very well be a mole from the enemy's camp, where satan has legions of demons to dispatch solely for the purpose of bringing about your spiritual destruction. Satan puts people in our path to entice us into idolatry to achieve his own selfish devices—so that he will get the glory out of our lives, instead of God. Can we conquer this thing? Do you ask yourself, "How can I put this man out? How can I stop being with this woman when she satisfies such critical needs? How can I stop letting this child rule my world? Am I out of control?" Oh, it takes a godly determination to prevail against the subtle, but real, fleshly idols drawn up by the cravings of the imagination under the influence of satan. Make a declaration to trust God! Can you beat this idolatry thing? Yes! There is victory for Spirit filled believers! Paul broke it down very plainly. "Nay, in all these things, we are more than conquerors through Him that loved us. For I am persuaded, that neither death, nor life, nor angels, nor principalities, nor powers, nor things present, nor things to come, nor height, nor depth, nor any creature, shall be able to separate us from the love of God, which is in Christ Jesus our Lord" (Rom. 8:38-39). Oh, Praise God and give Him the glory for your release right now! Hallelujah!

Satan knows within us lies a craving for power over others. He has studied human nature longer than we have studied his nature, so he caters to our desire for power. Satan pulls every slick trick out of his slimy bag to convince us that we should rule and control ourselves and others, without having to answer to anyone for our actions, or being held accountable in any way. Listen within. Do you hear echoes of "Who's wearing the pants in this house?" or "If it weren't for me, where would you be?" or "I make more money than you, so recognize who's running things here!" Sisters and brothers, be assured of one thing. There *will* be a day of reckoning. "For it is written, As I live, saith the Lord, every knee shall bow to me, and every tongue shall confess to God. So then, every one of us shall give account of himself to God" (Rom. 14:11,12). The Word of God is clear on this point. Satan knows chapter and verse, and now we must remind him at the time of temptation that we also know the Scriptures, and that we remain steadfast, unmovable and determined to walk in the Spirit and live in accordance with the knowledge, enlightenment and empowerment that God's Word provides. Guess what satan will do? That surly buzzard will get lost! How can we be so sure of it? The truth is recorded. "Submit yourselves therefore to God. Resist the devil, and he will flee from you" (James 4:7). The devil is once again defeated, Hallelujah!

Satan understands we have a longing for pleasure, so he tries to deify it within us. He influences us to seek pleasure instead of God, regardless of the associated risks or costs. Satan knows we have unmet passions, because he has programmed them within us, driving us to be exploited physically, emotionally, volitionally, economically, politically, socially, vocationally and mentally. Satan realizes that we yearn for approval or approbation, therefore he feeds that part of our being, making us gods in our own eyes. Satan realizes that our flesh desires to be popular, well known and revered; therefore, he attempts to fuel the zeal within, causing us to exalt ourselves and belittle others. He knows our appetite for money, houses, cars, clothes, etc., and he attempts to make these items priorities in our lives. Satan fiercely whips up these material images within the creative imaginations of our mind. If he can tempt us to worship and serve material possessions as gods, then he sets us up for the fall from grace and removes us from the ark of safety we find in God.

Satan inserts his acts and desires in the thoughts of the mind and then allows the imagination to handle all of the logistics (the who, the what, the when, the why, the where and the how). In Proverbs 7:6-27, the Bible unfolds a wonderful illustration of how the crafty harlot used her imagination to design and set up the capture of her prey. The harlot's imagination revealed the what in her plan, that is to wound, seduce, slay and kill the young devoid of understanding (vs. 10, 23, 26, 27). The harlot's imagination revealed the why of her imagination, to lead one astray and separate him from God (vs. 21, 25, 27). The imagination knew who it would prey on, the simple, void of understanding (v. 7). The imagination knew when it would attempt to implement its plan, in the twilight, in the evening, in the dark and black night (v. 9). The imagination, under satan's influence, planned where it would open up its plot—she would not abide in the house, but without, now in the streets, lying in wait at every corner (vs. 11, 12). Finally, her imagination discloses the how in her scheme, dressing seductively, pursuing and kissing with a sassy, lengthy, alluring appeal, until he yields to her desires (vs. 10, 13-22). The imagination is the tool used by satan to coordinate the plotting and scheming of the thought(s) and activity. Don't you remember how the imagination was used to coordinate and facilitate our sinful deeds? You do remember that special date, don't you? Do you remember how the imagination had you to place the call to him/her, and coordinate the rendezvous at the hotel, room 227, at 8:00 p.m.? Isn't it amazing how the imagination created the romantic atmosphere with champagne or wine and cheese? The imagination fantasized the bubble bath and lingerie on the marble, candlelit tub. It was the imagination that eagerly and expectantly planned hours of fun and enjoyment. You remember how you schemed to get out of the house, for whatever reason necessary, in order to attend the party, meet up with some friends, smoke a cigarette or one of those funny cigarettes, drink a beer or some liquor, go to the movies, stop by the store, visit your girlfriend or boyfriend, link up with the other man or woman, go play golf, shoot hoops or pool, and return the clothes you had no business buying anyway? Satan was busy then, and is busy now plotting, planning and sketching out strategies and tactics to draw believers into sin.

Satan started the imagination of Cain to commit murder against his own brother, Abel. Cain met a dreadful fate, banned and marked for life (Gen. 4:1-16). Judas' imagination caused him to plot to betray Jesus only to end up committing suicide (Matt. 26:14-16; Luke 22:3-6; Matt. 27:3-5). Jacob's imagination moved him to scheme against Laban, only to have it backfire on him (Gen. 30:22-31:2). The imaginations of Joseph's brothers led them to believe they could put out the dreams of the dreamer, only to later bow down to him (Gen. 37-47).

As we can see, the imagination can be used to conspire against anyone at anytime, depending on its availability and condition. According to the Scriptures, the imagination can affect four major areas of our lives:

1. our *walk* or lifestyle (Jer. 3:17);

2. our counsel is darkened, and frustrates God's purpose for our lives and impacts our *decision making capabilities* (Jer. 7:24);

3. our *thought life* throughout the day (Psalms 38:12, 62:3, 140:2);

4. our *behavior* (Gen. 11:6).

Because the imagination has such a tremendous impact on our lives, we must keep it under subjection; otherwise, it will lead us into Step Four, "Stirring of the Emotions".

Chapter Five
Step 4: Stirring of the Emotions

The fourth step common to temptation is the *stirring of the emotions*. This Chapter will focus on temptation reaching the innermost lusts and desires which are deeply embedded in our emotions. We will also learn how the first three steps combine with step four, *stirring of the emotions*, to bear heavily against the will of man. Are you ready? Good! Let's pause a moment to give God praise and thanks.

> Oh, Hallelujah! Father, we Thank You, Lord for revealing Your Word to us this day. We *love* You, *worship* and *adore* You! We sincerely enter Your gates with Praise and Thanksgiving! We come before You to ask that Your Presence closely abide near us, with us and in us. We look to You now for a fresh anointing as we seek a closer walk with You. Please open our hearts and minds, Lord, and increase our understanding of these revelations. We appreciate Your Word and Your many blessings, Lord, and we will faithfully give You the Praise. In the Name of Jesus, Amen!

Let's continue to dissect the methods of the enemy's operations against us. Satan reaches our emotions through the open doors of our senses. Once he has an open line to operate, he links our thought provoked minds to our vivid imaginations, and then he's ready for prime time! The setting is perfect for him to move to his next step—to stir up the lusts within our emotions.

The combination of the open door (senses), the mind engaged, the creative imagination, and the swirling emotions are the dynamics working to break down the will to cause it to yield to temptation and ultimately commit sin. We must not underestimate the power and predictability of satan's attack! Are you familiar with the tiles in the game of Dominos? Each tile is thick enough to stand alone; however when Domino tiles are stacked closely together, they stand in that inert state until given a little tap. After the impetus of the tap, all the tiles fall down in rapid succession. We call this phenomenon "the domino effect"! Satan's embattlement works in exactly the same manner. The senses alone stand in our bodies to receive and process information. They stand independently to serve their functions. The mind is powerful. Our brain transmits and regulates the nerve center of our bodies. The mind is an amazing organ where thought is processed. The mind is essential for our existence, having a profound impact on our entire being. The imagination is awesome! Without it, we would walk around in an uncreative, dull existence. In and of itself, the imagination is extraordinary, sparking great visionaries to realize their dreams. Human emotions are fascinating. Without them, we would be confused about how to appropriately respond to feelings, e.g., happiness, sadness, joy, pain, anger and fear. The senses, the mind, the imagination and the emotions are needed, necessary and important human functions. Where's the danger? We're under constant attack. Satan makes it his business to disturb our Christian walk by "tapping" the senses, mind, imagination and emotions. Every waking opportunity, the enemy will "tap" the senses with temptation to begin the "domino effect" through our thoughts, and then the satanic influenced imagination makes its downward spiral to ripple through our lusts to stir up the emotions. The force of the "domino effect" picks up steam now as the senses, mind, imagination and emotions weigh heavily against the will. When the will weakens from the pressure, it is subject to collapse. The collective strength mounted against the will can diminish its ability to say "yes" to Jesus and "no" to temptation. Should the will completely yield to the temptation, the fall is complete, and sin and separation from God result. My Lord! We don't have to take the fall when we are in Christ. It is important to know the process of temptation, and how one weak link or careless "tap" can destroy the believer's fellowship with God.

"But every man is tempted, when he is drawn away of his own *lust*" (James 1:14). Lust, *epithumia* in the Greek language, denotes a strong desire of any kind. In our study, we make reference to lust in the negative sense, the evil lusts of the flesh or the good (but not godly) lusts of the soul that are contrary or inconsistent to the will of God. Remember in Matthew 16:22, how Peter expressed his desire for Jesus to bypass the road to the cross? This desire or lust was a good one albeit contrary to the will of God for the lives of Jesus and His bride, the church. Note, James is led to label lusts as "his own", readily claiming ownership. James speaks of the lusts that have been ingrained and built into the sinful nature (the flesh) of the individual over time, and have taken up residency, refusing to change their address, even when served notice to vacate.

In Chapter One, we studied satan's method of programming sinful desires into the mind and heart of man. We exposed his tactics, using a technology analogy, where satan is the systems engineer and our heart and mind comprise the operating system (or hard drive) of the computer. Let's revisit that process. Satan routinely downloads his passions, obsessions and infatuations into the databases of our hearts, so that the information can be retrieved and uploaded to our minds, and then exported into the next recipient's mind, mailbox or database. These imported desires come from external sources (objectively) and become longings that can be uploaded or internalized from the heart into the mind (subjectively) in a moment of time. Have you ever wondered where those sinful cravings come from? Why do they seem to surface at the most inopportune times? How do they become so pervasive? Sinful urges can take over our thought life, our plans for the day, weekend and lives. According to James 1:14, the longings come from the lust harbored from within. These lusts have become embedded chips within the innermost recesses of our mind and being.

In John 8:44, the Bible teaches us that satan, the father and author of the flesh and its appetites, reproduces his lusts or desires into the old man, or the sinful nature, to produce the works of the flesh in man. Satan's program is advanced through our lusts. He has observed us since we were born, so he is familiar with our strengths and weaknesses. Satan continues to cipher lusts into our hearts so he will be able to persistently seduce or entrap us into desiring the forbidden fruits of the world. He delights in our terrible jams. Satan knows all about our fleshly, selfish cravings, because he is the author of these negative appetites into our beings. These lusts are always lurking within us, awaiting opportunity to be stirred and manifested. We should know that the Bible is saturated with descriptive accounts of lusts and their places of origin:

1) "Worldly lusts"—Titus 2:12
2) "Lusts of the soul"—Rev. 18:14
3) "Sin's lusts"—Rom. 6:12

4) "Heart's lusts"—Psalm 81:12
5) "Fleshly lusts"—Gal. 5:16
6) "Lusts of other men"—I Peter 4:12
7) "Lusts of the flesh"—I John 2:16
8) "Youthful lusts"—II Tim. 2:22

The Bible also describes the nature and activity of these lusts:

1) "Sexual lusts"—Rom. 1:27
2) "Lusts after one's beauty"—Prov. 6:25
3) "Covetous lusts"—Rom. 7:7
4) "Corrupting lusts"—II Peter 1:4
5) "Unclean lusts"—II Peter 2:10
6) "Lusts after evil things"—I Cor. 10:6
7) "Deceitful lusts"—Eph. 4:22
8) "Ungodly lusts"—Jude 1:18
9) "Divers lusts"—II Tim. 3:6
10) "Hurtful and foolish lusts"—I Tim. 6:8
11) "Warring lusts"—James 4:1
12) "Extreme lusts"—I Thess. 4:5

This is not an exhaustive list of the lusts that satan authors, but an illuminating slate to reveal his internal temperaments and external liveliness. Satan does not want us to know how he entangles us in his web of temptations. We must understand how he maneuvers from the outside in if we are going to understand how he then in cooperation with our lusts, works from the inside out.

The heart gives birth to lust when we allow a natural, godly desire to become an unrestrained, uncontrollable fleshly idol. Lust is more than just an inappropriate sexual desire. It can be an unnatural, greedy yearning for *anything* (possessions, power, position, money, influence over people, knowledge, or even sports and endorsements). When one becomes so preoccupied with someone or something until it affects their decisions and perspective on life, desire has given birth to lust. Lust is a powerful tool used by the enemy to convert God-given appetites and desires into hellish, irrepressible, fleshly longings. Lust is an overwhelming passion that sends one's nature into a torrential whirlwind, totally out of control! After thieves see an enviable prize, they invite into the mind the imagination's creativity. The cycle spins by stirring up the lusts, and the act of thievery soon follows.

Why do we as believers sometimes feel alone in this battle against our emotions? Do we not realize satan presses us with that demon of loneliness only when we allow him the slightest opening? The nature of the enemy is to tempt us. "Be sober, be vigilant; because your adversary the devil, as a roaring lion, walketh about, seeking whom he may devour" (I Peter 5:8). We have all the ammunition we need to turn satan's menacing roar into a docile meow, *if* that! Our weapon of choice is the Word of God! Hallelujah! Follow the lead of Jesus in the wilderness, and beat satan *down* with the Sword of the Spirit! When we hear the voice of satan whisper:

> "Oh, come on, it couldn't hurt to touch it, or even take it. It looks mighty good, and after *all*, who's looking?"

Counter that devil with:

> "Get behind me satan! You have no hold on me here in this place THIS day, for the Bible tells me in the Book of Joshua, Chapters 6 and 7, that Brother Achan has already walked down this path before me! God com-

> manded Achan not to touch the spoils of Jericho, and the Word says Achan not only touched the good looking clothes, silver and gold, but he took them and hid them in his tent. That thief died for his sin of disobedience, so satan get OUT of my way with this temptation because I want to LIVE!! Satan, I come against you right now with the blood of the Lamb. I rebuke you in the name of Jesus! Get behind me!!"

That's it!! Speak **boldly** in the face of satan's attack! Counter every demonic force with the authority of the Word of God! Hallelujah!! "Resist the devil, and he will flee from you" (James 4:7). But remember Jesus' experience in the wilderness? He was counterpunched by satan. Expect it! The docile little meow of the enemy only lasts for a season, and that season could be in the instant of a split second or stretched out over a period of years before the roar threatens again. Expect satan to return with a smooth line:

> "Well, don't' be confused. Achan was living under the law. This is a new day under the dispensation of grace. Nobody throws stones. That is barbaric. You will not die if you take it! Not this time. Go ahead. Enjoy! Live a little!"

Where's your weapon? Thank the Lord for His Word! Speak **boldly**:

> "Satan, you tried this move on Ananias and Sapphira in the Book of Acts, Chapter 5. They attempted to rob God of what rightfully belonged to Him because their lusts for

> money were stronger than their love for God. Ananias and Sapphira coveted their gains more than they feared God, and it cost them their lives! In the Gospel of John, 14:15, Jesus said, 'If ye love me, keep my commandments.' Satan, is there any part of that you do NOT understand? I am determined to be in the will of God! I Rebuke you satan, in the name of Jesus!

Victory is attainable. We must conquer satan daily with the Word! Remember, the enemy knows Scripture also, so be prepared for the comeback of his quotes *and misquotes*. Spiritual warfare is a constant battle. The lusts of our flesh will sink us every time. Our nature is to seek warmth, beauty, safety and enjoyment. Without a strong foundation in the Word, these fineries will come masked in non-threatening sheep's clothing, and eventually cost us the expense of our spirit, soul and body. My Lord! "Thy Word have I hid in mine heart, that I might not sin against thee" (Psalm 119:11).

In II Samuel 13:1-19, there is a story of a man named Amnon. He loved his sister, Tamar, so much that it vexed his soul. She was beautiful, well configured, and a virgin. Amnon longed after her essence. Amnon had a devious friend, Jonadab, with whom he conspired a sinister plot to rape his sister. Upon Tamar's arrival, Amnon took hold of her and told her to lay with him, but she refused him. Then his savage, ferocious lusts led to a hostile takeover of his members (his hands, his mouth and his strength) which led to his attacking Tamar's body. He forced himself on her, and then his lust for her turned into great hatred. Unmanageable lusts within our hearts require immediate satisfaction and gratification, and satan desires to help us fulfill them both.

Lust demands its own way, and will scheme and plot until it wins. If only we could have warned Amnon about the perilous risks associated with sinful gratification. It is foolish to win temporal battles and lose eternal life! "For what shall it profit a man, if he shall gain the whole world, and lose his own soul?" (Mark 8:36) Believers should be keenly aware how lusts impact our spiritual growth and development, and know that yielding to satan's devices causes us to walk according to the flesh, and *not* the Spirit.

Prior to our acceptance of Christ, satan was building in our hearts and lives lustful desires, mercurial feelings and idolatrous affections for whatever thoughts we processed. Initially, satan builds in the heart, in our fleshly nature, lustful desires through the senses, the mind and the imagination. After our acceptance of Christ, the lusts or desires programmed within our nature have the ability from within to draw us away from walking in the Spirit and heeding God's commands. When satan desires to lead a believer astray, he uses external means, something, someone or someplace to mate with the internal desire, affection or feeling that he has ingrained in us, to mate with each other and cause us to give birth to failure or to fall into temptation.

In step four of the eight deadly steps in a temptation involving our lusts, remember there is the objective side as well as the subjective side. The objective side represents that person, place, thing or event that appeals to our senses (externally). The subjective represents those feelings, desires, appetites, affections, cravings, etc., (internally) that have become a part of our response system and experiences over time. The Apostle James helps us understand from the subjective or experiential viewpoint, that when we are drawn away, it is through the awakening of the indwelling lust that we possess (his own lust) and enjoy objects of temptation. The arousing of lust is through something or someone we have entertained in our minds and pictured in our imaginations. The stimulation of lust begins with what we have seen with our eyes, smelled with our noses, touched with our body parts, heard with our ears or tasted with our mouths. Often, our memories will recall to our minds someone or something causing the resurrection of those sinful appetites and yearnings. Sitting at our desks, walking down the streets, glancing through a picture album, hearing a name called, smelling a certain cologne or perfume, passing by a restaurant, cruising in a familiar car or traveling to a certain park can invoke memories to rekindle flames long ago extinguished. We become overwhelmed in thought. Thought? What types of thoughts? Thoughts about reliving those intimate moments with an ex-girlfriend or boyfriend, or ex-wife or ex-husband.... Thoughts about owning cars and houses we cannot afford, but are willing to do whatever it takes to get them..... Thoughts about stealing money from the church, the elderly or from a parent to purchase jewelry or pay for a drug habit..... Thoughts of stealing answers for a test to ensure a passing grade in a class..... Thoughts of rationalization, e.g., reasoning that it is okay to desire people, places and things more than God. We attempt to justify lustfully provoked thoughts:

> "It's okay to covet my neighbor's wife, house or car. It's okay to lie in order to get a job because the need for money should make it acceptable. It's alright for me to set up my co-workers in order to get their jobs and their salaries. It's okay if I deceive my husband or wife, son or daughter, mother or

father, employer or co-worker, pastor or church in order to protect self from exposure of past failures or current mistakes."

The memory, reasoning and/or imagination can cause an intense eruption of our lusts to take place within us if we have not dealt with them via the cross of Jesus. Draw power from what the Word of God says: "And they that are Christ's have crucified the flesh with the affections and lusts" (Gal. 5:24). Daily, believers are engaged in the struggle to kill the flesh. Through it all, we can surely stand against the enemy if we are mindful of one important question: "Do we belong to Christ?" Be confident that Christ is our Keeper, and boldly respond in the affirmative. "Yes, indeed! Through Christ we can overcome!" Hallelujah!

We benefit by being well acquainted with satan's methods because familiarity brings on predictability. If we know satan's angle, then we can effectively defend his shots. For too long we have generalized in our preaching and teaching on temptations, but now it is time for the Body of Christ, through the anointing of God's Spirit, to dismember what satan does not want us to learn! It is time to stop falling prey to the enemy's disguises! It is high time for us to stop overlooking TEMPTATION, the one weapon in the enemy's arsenal that hinders and stops believers from entering into their sense of purpose and destiny of fulfilling God's will for their lives. If we are going to live for God, and not for satan, we must heighten our awareness of his manipulative enterprise.

We should be reaching a place in our study of this book where the steps of a temptation are being revealed and retained. Can you quote the process? Well, let's review it again. Once the senses are stimulated and the seed of temptation is sown in our mind, the imagination is influenced and proceeds to stir up our inner lusts (feelings, affections and desires). Satan continues to fling his steps of temptation to gain greater access into the second faculty of the human soul, the emotions. Satan knows that most believers tend to be carnal versus spiritual! He takes full advantage of the fact that we are emotionally driven. If the truth be told, most individuals who have not been broken and strengthened by God's Spirit live, move and exist by their natural emotions, mortal passions, carnal lusts and sensual appetites. Once satan flashes a thought from our senses onto the screens of our minds, and the imagination paints a beautiful picture, he wants us to buy in to what we see and feel. Satan desires to have the emotions delight in viewing what the imagination has designed, developed and presented to our minds by creating an emotional attachment to the thoughts placed in our minds. If the imagination does its job of depicting the thoughts sown in our minds as something desirable or worthwhile, sweet to the nostrils, sensual to the touch, appetizing to the taste, appealing to the eyes and melodious to the ears, then it strengthens the possibility of stirring the emotions within, to partner with the thoughts sown, causing the will to be weakened and yield to the temptation.

Throughout this text, we continue to study the scene of the first recorded temptation. The story of Adam and Eve has been told in our schools and homes since we were children. The topic of temptation is intriguing, and the Garden of Eden has inspired many writers, producers and advertisers to capitalize on its appeal. However, there is danger in taking these events lightly! If we are not careful, believers as well as unbelievers will have the tendency to discount the severity of what happened that fateful day when the serpent tempted Sister Eve. Revisiting the "scene of the crime" allows us to investigate the forensic evidence satan always leaves behind.

His fingerprints are *made*, and it is important that we keep them on file so we can easily identify him and call him OUT from his spot in a lineup, and keep that rascal bound! Let's take a closer look at the scene by pausing to read Genesis 3:1-7. The written record is beneficial at this point.

Verse 1: Now the serpent was more subtle than any beast of the field which the Lord had made. And he said unto the woman, Yea, hath God said Ye shall not eat of every tree in the garden?

Verse 2: And the woman said unto the serpent, We may eat of the fruit of the trees of the garden:

Verse 3: But of the fruit of the tree which is in the midst of the garden, God hath said, Ye shall not eat of it, neither shall ye touch it, lest ye die.

Verse 4: And the serpent said unto the woman, Ye shall not surely die:

Verse 5: For God doth know that in the day that ye eat thereof, then your eyes shall be opened, and ye shall be as gods, knowing good and evil.

Verse 6: And when the woman saw that the tree was good for food, and that it was pleasant to the eyes, and a tree to be desired to make one wise, she took of the fruit thereof, and did eat, and gave also unto her husband with her; and he did eat.

Verse 7: And the eyes of them both were opened, and they knew that they were naked; and they sewed fig leaves together, and made themselves aprons.

The account in the Garden so clearly outlines the eight steps satan uses in a temptation. He first appears on the scene and begins talking to Eve. She not only hears satan, but she also listens to him as he draws her attention to the tree. How did he get in? He gained access through her senses, and then began the "mind" game. Satan spoke those lies, and had that woman believing God was mistaken, and that He didn't really mean what He said! In that instant, Satan convinced Eve that she would not die, but turn into a little god herself. My Lord! The tragedy is that she allowed satan to sow seeds of doubt in her mind about the Word of God. He then cranked up the imagination's engine, generating within her a lust for what she had seen and heard. The Holy Spirit reveals to us how the serpent's words activated Eve's emotions. In verse 3, after Eve acknowledged the Word of God, in verses 4 and 5, the serpent painted both a wonderful and disastrous picture for all of mankind. Read verse 6 and note how he stimulated her senses and increased her interest in the tree by speaking word pictures in her mind. Remember "the domino effect"? The combined weight of Eve's stimulated senses, satan influenced thoughts, tainted imagination and lustful emotions, caused so much pressure on her will, that she soon yielded her will as she touched and tasted the forbidden fruit. Her sin cast all humanity outside of relationship and fellowship with God! We all come from Father Adam and Mother Eve, and satan sows his thoughts and attempts to make our thoughts his thoughts exactly as he did with *mom* and *dad*.

Through the world system and the things of the world, the people of the world, and even fellow Christians, satan sets up believers to fall into emotional pitfalls. He knows how to get our attention! Satan has the ability to set up the suitable atmosphere and environment to perk up our interest, and he arranges the necessary props in order to accomplish his feat. He hires the right actors to perform in the scenes in his movies. He then directs the set, calling out "Lights! Camera! Action!" Satan choreographed Judas' betrayal of Jesus by playing on his emotions (Luke 22:1-6). Satan set up the atmosphere by creating tension between Jesus and the Chief Priests and Scribes around The Feast of Unleavened Bread or the Passover (Matthew 26: 1-5). If satan was able to direct the betrayal of our Lord (within God's limitations), then he is also able to wield ruin and devastation to every believer within God's limitations (Job 1,2).

We can not over emphasize the importance of understanding frame by frame the tactics satan uses in a temptation. We have spent time under the anointing of God's Spirit analyzing and dissecting these Biblical truths to get us to this point in our study. Satan is incensed right now because we are learning his strategies for causing believers to fall. I don't know about you, but I am glad there is victory in growing in the grace and in the knowledge of God's Word.

> "Oh my God, help us to see and understand that if we do not take the time to know satan and his strategies for tempting believers, we will live a life of defeat and

failure, one of heartache and pain and one of struggles and continual strife. Help us to see that yielding to temptation is not a part of your divine will for our lives, but joy and peace, love and prosperity, salvation and glorification, in Jesus' name we pray. Amen."

Once the enemy secures our attention, captures our consciousness, invigorates our imaginations and arouses our emotions, then he leads us into Step Five, "The Succumbing of the Will".

Chapter Six
Step 5: The Succumbing of the Will

The fifth step common to temptation is the *succumbing of the will.* To succumb means to weaken, and we all know how it feels to be weakened. Where do we turn when we feel as if a feather could tip us over? When we are embattled, beaten to a pulp by satan, and on the brink of the fall, to whom should we go? "God is our refuge and strength, a very present help in trouble" (Psalm 46:1). Turning to God and holding fast to His Word is the Answer! The Word of God flows like a river through this text to reveal the steps common to temptation. "But every man is tempted, when he is drawn away of his own lust, *and enticed*" (James 1:14). It is amazing to know how latent with revelation this Scripture is about the process of temptation, so we continue to focus on this verse. The Word clearly states that we are *all* tempted—*every* man. In Chapter Two, we closely examined the process of being drawn *away* from the Spirit of God. In Chapter Five, we noted how James was led to label lusts as "his own", claiming ownership and the internal condition of the fleshly nature.

In this Chapter, we will further focus on this Biblical revelation found in James 1:14. What comes to mind when we hear the word "enticed"? Does it invoke tempting, alluring and seductive thoughts? Enticed, (in the Greek, *deleazo*), means to "lure by a bait". The Word of God reveals to us how the enemy of our souls dangles before us something or someone capable of whetting our appetites to incite our emotions. He suspends before us, like a fisherman hangs a worm on his hook to catch a fish, that thing or person who can cause us to nibble away, and eventually bite, while we, like the fish, are unaware we are hooked! The bait looks alive and real, but more often than not, it is artificial and counterfeit. James chose use of the word "enticed" to show its relationship to the word "lust". As lusts within the heart become overpowering, they generate the process whereby the will of the human soul begins to succumb or weaken to the thoughts and desires of the flesh. According to Ephesians 2:2-3, at some point in time, we were all influenced by the prince of the power of the air, and that we all lived, moved and had our very existence in the lusts of our flesh, fulfilling or acting out the desires of the flesh and the mind. Paul received revelatory knowledge that our lifestyles were influenced and shaped by satan. He also was inspired to reveal that the expressions of our wills were heavily impacted by the lusts of the flesh (body) and the lusts of the mind (soul).

What makes man a unique creation of God is that he has a will. The will is the organ of decision, which enables us to choose to walk in Christ or in darkness. Temptation puts a constant stress on the will, causing "the domino effect". It presses the weight of the senses and the mind's thoughts and imagination against inward fleshly desires to stir up lustful emotions. As lusts intensify, they begin to pressure the will to yield to fleshly desires. We have seen in the previous chapter that lusts can originate from the world, the heart, the soul, the flesh, sin and from other people. Once originated, lusts can reproduce themselves within us. The external or internal demand forced on us by stirred up lusts always requires a response from us. How we respond to the pressure determines whether the strain is strengthened or weakened, whether we succumb to the evil forces of satan or prevail victoriously in Christ. When the weight of the senses, thoughts, imagination and emotions are pressing against our will, and our knees begin to buckle to surrender our will to satan, we must reach out to a Higher Power for quick intervention in order to stay the course! At that moment, it is time to call on the Lord of salvation! This is that critical juncture when we feel as if the pressure cooker top is either about to explode or get that necessary adjustment of temperance in order to cook a perfectly simmered dish. This is the moment when the landing gear either drops down steadily or gets stuck for a crash landing. The weakening of the will can be compared to the moments of stress we experience during a trip that requires air travel. Sometimes we enjoy the convenience of nonstop or direct flights, and at other times, we must make connections requiring long layovers. There are many variables—the trip can be long or short, with or without turbulence, day or night. There is pressure, and the unknown is a little disconcerting. "Who's in the cockpit? Is there a federal sky marshall on this flight? Could we get there already?" As the pressure of life's circumstances intensifies, our will begins to buckle.

We should do all that we can to refuse satan's temptations before we find ourselves "knee deep" in step 5, *the succumbing (weakening) of the will.* There is so much pressure when we allow satan to infiltrate our "inner man". Why "put yourself in harm's way" by stepping right into a situation that you *know* is trouble on the temptation front? Help Lord! Why place yourself in such a compromising position? Know that satan is out to destroy you, so avoid his path! The answer is in Christ.

Satan must gain access to the will of man if he is going to cause mankind to work with him in partnership to fulfill his dark and dastardly deeds. Satan must gnaw away at the will until eventually there is the capitulation of the will. His overriding objective is to weaken then seize the will of the believer. Isaiah 14:12 reveals that although Lucifer (satan) had been cut down to the ground, he still possessed enough wherewithal to weaken the wills of the nations or the people. Because he cannot force mankind to obey him, he works on him (opening the senses), against him (opposing the mind and imagination) and in him (through the lusts) through whatever means necessary (trials, storms, relationships, etc.) until we say "uncle". Satan is lowdown—the author of confusion! He will send multiple thoughts to our minds, ask innumerable questions to defy all logic, and send feelings up and down the sine waves of our life. Satan gets off on shaking our relationships and destroying harmonious fellowship. He sows seeds to cause us to think we are losing our mind, and fans the flames of discouragement when peace should abound. The enemy presents opportunities for sin and failure, until finally, one day, at the appointed time, we succumb to his will. His ultimate desire is to make us vulnerable and defenseless to his schemes. He tries to wear our wills down and away so that when he displays before us or makes mention to us what he wishes, we bow down and fall prey to his attempt. Now we know why Proverbs 4:23 declares emphatically, "Keep thy heart with all diligence; for out of it are the issues of life". If we allow satan access to our hearts, we allow him access to our lives. Now we can understand why Proverbs 23:26 proclaims, "My Son, give me thine heart...", because there is another force which seeks to steal, kill and destroy our hearts and our lives. Listen to the Word according to Joshua 24:14-15:

> "Now therefore fear the Lord, and serve him in sincerity and in truth: and put away the gods which your fathers served on the other side of the flood, and in Egypt; and serve ye

> the Lord. And if it seem evil unto you to serve the Lord, choose you this day whom ye will serve; whether the gods which your fathers served that were on the other side of the flood, or the gods of the Amorites, in whose land ye dwell: but as for me and my house, we will serve the Lord".

Joshua received insight about the importance of the *will* in choosing life or death, God or satan, riches or poverty, honor or dishonor, health or sickness. If we allow the enemy to succeed in breaking down our wills, we will end up serving the gods of this world—those we served before we accepted Christ. Such mistakes please satan and grieve the Holy Spirit.

Let's take a look at several scriptural examples of satan's attack on mankind's will. By now, we have become scholars on the origin of temptation. We know that it all started in the Garden of Eden! Remember the serpent's conversation with Eve? (Gen. 3:1-6) He allured and seduced her with his deceptive words and lying tongue, until finally, she succumbed to his will. Remember, when the enemy invites us into a conversation, that we should be careful. Once he starts speaking through those pretty lips or that rock hard jowl, words so very smooth, gentle, and congenial, he will not stop until he gets what he wants!!

In Genesis 13:1-11, Abram and Lot were preparing to part their ways when Lot fixed his eyes upon the plain of Jordan. Jordan was well watered, even as the garden of the Lord or the land of Egypt. As he looked into the eyes of death and destruction, he was baited by what he *thought* he saw, only to live to regret his decision. Let's look at II Peter 2:7-9:

Verse 7: And delivered just Lot, vexed with the filthy conversation of the wicked:

Verse 8: (For that righteous man dwelling among them, in seeing and hearing, vexed his righteous soul from day to day with their unlawful deeds;)

Verse 9: The Lord knoweth how to deliver the godly out of temptations, and to reserve the unjust unto the day of judgment to be punished:

This reference discloses that Lot's soul (his mind, will and emotions) was vexed, weakened and damaged through his senses by the influences in his environment. His atmosphere, environment and associates demoralized his will, discouraged his heart, and corrupted his lifestyle to the point that he had to be delivered out of his situation. Have you ever been there? Has your will to do good ever been bound by your will to perform evil? Have you ever experienced Romans 7:15-21? Have you ever been so deeply entrenched in a mess that you could not get out of it by yourself? But isn't it a blessing to know that God knows how and when to deliver us out of our mess? Give Him great praise! Hallelujah!!

In Genesis 25:29-34, we find the story of Jacob and Esau — the twin brothers born to Isaac and Rebekah. Let's review what happened. Jacob was in the kitchen cooking when Esau returned home faint from working in the fields. Esau could smell the aroma of the food, so he tracked the scent to the pot on the stove. As he smelled that food, his hunger pains increased and he became disarmed of his willpower and vulnerable to any request. He asked his brother for some food, and Jacob took advantage of Esau's hunger by offering him a trade—his birthright (the blessing of the oldest son) for the food. You know the rest of the story! Esau sold out! He succumbed his will to the natural, at the expense of possessing the supernatural!! Have you ever been there? Have you ever sold out your Christianity for a season of sin and so called pleasure? Has your fleshly appetite ever reached the point that it took over your spiritual appetite, causing you to forget your birthright and all the possessions and inheritance associated with it? Have you ever for the sake of temporary pleasure laid down your religion, laid down your values, and laid down your position in heavenly places? If so? Welcome to the club of "*Been* There, *Done* That"! It's a mighty crowded establishment!!

In Joshua 7:19-26, the Holy Spirit reveals another historical account of an individual whose will succumbed to temptation. In fact, we have made a case study of the sin of Achan in this book. As we have learned, Brother Achan did not help himself. He and the rest of the children of Israel received explicit instructions not to touch or take anything out of the conquered city of Jericho, or they would be cursed (Joshua 6:18-19). However, Achan, even after hearing the warning, made a fatal blunder. He did not obey the commandment of the Lord. The Bible says "he saw the garments, the silver and the gold, and coveted them". We can only imagine that he began to desire and think about how fashionable, stylish and chic he would appear in his new wardrobe. He no doubt mused about how much money he would have to spend on the town wining and dining his wife, family and friends. As he imagined all of these festivities taking place in his life, he became excited beyond control, until his will broke down, and he blew it!! Have you ever been prohibited from something or someone, but after seeing the object of your affection, you could not control yourself, and *had* to have it, no matter what it cost you? …and DID it cost you? Have you ever touched that which was marked "Do not Touch"? Have your fingers ever done the walking, while the enemy did the talking? Have your senses, your thoughts, your imagination and your lusts ever teamed up against you and beat you down to the ground? That is what happened to Achan and still happens to us today. We will be troubled repeatedly unless we study to show ourselves approved unto God in the area of temptations!

Nehemiah found favor in the eyes of God (Neh. 2:18). When Nehemiah heard the wall of Jerusalem was destroyed in battle, he fasted, wept and prayed for God's forgiveness over the sins of his fathers (Neh. 1:4-11). Nehemiah was a servant, a cupbearer to the king. He asked and received the king's blessing to go to Judah to rebuild the wall (Neh. 2:5). Nehemiah gained favor with the king and the King of Kings! Hallelujah! Have you ever enjoyed divine favor when you KNEW that God was with you and your steps were ordered? Was everybody happy for you? Do not be surprised when everyone doesn't rejoice with you. Some might even try to trip you. If so, you should know that you are not alone. Be encouraged and watch this! There were three men, Sanballat, Tobiah and Geshem, the Arabian, who were among the enemies of Israel (Neh 6:1). They heard the wall was near completion, and being influenced by satan, attempted to block its final construction. They sent Nehemiah five letters to entrap him, harm him, weaken him and effectively impede his progress (Neh. 6:25). Because Nehemiah was in touch with God for *himself*, he knew to ignore their pleas and continue to walk in the anointing of God. When satan knocked, Nehemiah did not answer, and the vision of the wall was realized (Neh. 6:15). "Trust in the Lord with all thine heart; and lean not unto thine own understanding. In all thy ways acknowledge Him, and He shall direct thy paths" (Prov. 3:5-6). Let's learn from Nehemiah. Every message that appears to be in our best interest is *not* of God. Know His voice, and seek the mind of God to know His will.

Has God ever assigned a task to your hands and you were challenged to forsake the work and enter into covenant with the adversary? Have you ever told someone "no", and he or she kept asking you the same thing over and over again until you finally buckled and gave in? Brothers, have you ever tried to seduce a sister by taking her out to dinner, a movie, on a cruise or for a stroll in the park? Have you presented gifts, flowers, whispered sweet nothings in her ear, massaged her mind with soothing words, stroked her cheeks, kissed her hand, promised to attend church with her, intending to weaken her will until she finally succumbed to your will? Sisters, have you ever worn a revealing dress, bathed in enchanting oils, prepared the candlelit dinner, poured the wine, entertained with romantic music, batted or winked your eyes, painted your voluptuous lips with lipstick, communicated through your body language, to attract and entice Mr. Right? Sisters and brothers, have you ever been the recipient of such appealing activities? Well, if you have, you have experienced *first hand*, Step 6 in a temptation, *the succumbing of the will.* How many times has someone stroked and provoked you until you finally caved in to their requests? Has anyone ever so relentlessly sent to you message after message, placed phone call after phone call, forwarded email after e-mail, called your mother's house, your father's job, your sister's apartment, your brother's condominium, your girlfriend's townhouse, and even your boyfriend's pager trying to track you down so that you would finally yield to their dreams, bend to their hopes, and bow to their visions? Do you have any co-workers annoying you and working your last nerve to persuade and detract you from performing your tasks so that you can assist them with theirs? Do you know any Sanballat's, Geshem's or Tobiah's in your life? If so, look out! They do not have your best interest at heart, only theirs. If you know anyone who fits that description, the only way to respond to such underhanded chicanery is to respond as Nehemiah did. Stay focused and true to your calling from God!

In Genesis 39:7-20, Joseph, the Dreamer, experienced first hand an impetuous, appealing temptress in the person of Potiphar's wife. The wife of the Captain of the Guard in Pharoah's army fixed her eyes upon Joseph and became spellbound with his attractive features and his well favored prominence. As she slithered her way over to him, she spoke with such venom in her words that if any other man would hear them, perhaps he would have been bitten and ceded to her charm, but not Joseph! Potiphar's wife approached Joseph. "But he refused, and said unto his master's wife, Behold, my master wotteth not what is with me in the house, and he hath committed all that he hath to my hand; There is none greater in this house than I; neither hath he kept back any thing from me but thee, because thou art his wife: how then can I do this great wickedness, and sin against God?" (Gen. 39:7-8) Joseph spoke these antidotal words as Potiphar's wife moved towards him. He shifted his body out of her reach to position himself away from her touch. She was totally under the influence of satan as she deafened her ears to the sound of his words and continued to proceed after her target day by day (v. 10), refusing to quit or give in, hoping that sooner or later, Joseph's will would acquiesce to her temptation. "And it came to pass about this time, that Joseph went into the house to do his business; and there was none of the men of the house there within. And she caught him by his garment, saying, Lie with me: and he left his garment in her hand, and fled, and got him out" (vs. 11-12). These Scriptures reveal to us how she timed her attack against Joseph, showing how determined she was to drain him of his will power to "do the right thing". Have you ever been there? Can you identify with this situation? Do you know this lustful spirit that attached itself to Potiphar's wife? Have you ever been caught in a bad situation trying to do what is right? Have you ever been under the influence of this spirit? Have you ever tried to force yourself on someone who was not interested in you? Have you ever stood in the shoes of Joseph or Potiphar's wife? May God have mercy on our souls! Thank God we have Biblical accounts of individuals who knew the importance of running from the enemy.

The Book of Proverbs, chapter 7:6-21 draws our attention to a woman who was a harlot. The Bible describes her as being crafty, loud, fast, aggressive and rebellious. She was dressed to attract men, bold in her approach to seduce men, skillful in addressing and answering their every reply and objection. She was smooth at convincing and weakening them to succumb to her desires. "With her much fair speech she caused him to yield, with the flattering of her lips she forced him" (v. 21). This woman, symbolically, could represent a man or woman whose plan is to induce another into sexually immoral behavior. He or she can be found not only on the street corner, but also in the grocery store, at the mall, a house party, a theatrical play, an art showing, any given restaurant, on the job, a vacation cruise, while traveling on business, or even in the church!! Have you ever met this person in your life's journey? Have you ever wished you never had? Have you ever met someone who had an answer to your every objection? Do you ever wonder if "groupies" fall into this category? Have you ever played the harlot or the gullible one? What would or will you do differently having now studied the tricks and the trades of our foe? Are you taken by the cologne or perfume that you smell? Are you ensnared by the beauty of her face or the dashing looks he possesses? Do the dimples on the face, the wink of an eye or the gleam of the smile intrigue you? Be careful, you could be falling into the traps of the adversary!!

There was a woman from the valley of Sorek who won the heart of a man on top of a mountain in Hebron. In the Book of Judges, chapter 16:4-21, we find the story of Samson and Delilah, which is almost as well known as Adam and Eve. Samson was one of the physically strongest men in the Bible who fell in love with Delilah, a woman who sold him out for some money. Samson loved Delilah (v. 4), and his affection for her was known by the lords of the Philistines (v. 5). They approached her, enticed and bribed her to enter into an agreement with them. Each of the lords of the Philistines offered Delilah eleven hundred pieces of silver if she would disclose to them the source of Samson's strength. Samson, deafened by sweet words, and blinded by beauty and love, allowed Delilah to whisk her way into his presence and most candidly ask him for the source of his strength. Samson did not even realize his dilemma—that Delilah was not only his lover, but also his temptress. She was no longer after his love, heart and soul, but his life, head and strength. The Bible states in verses 6-15, that she persistently and aggressively sought after the key to Samson's strength. She was as driven as a child who refuses to take no for an answer, or a drug addict in search of his next fix. He kept playing with fire as if he could not be burned. "Can a man take fire in his bosom, and his clothes not be burned? Can one go upon hot coals, and his feet not be burned?" (Prov. 6:27-28) Samson continued to toy with the fiery darts delivered by Delilah. He continued to dabble with sin, continued to sleep with the enemy, and continued to add wood to the fire, until finally his soul became vexed unto death, so much so, that he told her all of his heart (vs. 16-17). He shared the secret to his anointing. He put into the hands of the enemy information that would ruin him for life. His inner man became accessible to the will of the enemy. He opened and allowed his archenemy to enter his house. All of his protective devices were dismantled, and the lords of the Philistines (through Delilah) conquered him. Wow! What a terrible tragedy! Have you ever been there? Are you a Delilah or a Samson? Are you using others to do evil as did the lords of the Philistines? Are politics your game, and ruining people your claim to fame? Do you start the fire or are you the keeper of the flames? Is money of greater value to you than friendship and trust? Do you believe that you are that strong in your self, that no weapon formed against you by the archenemy can stop you? Do you enjoy playing with fire, or would you dare to carry the torch? Satan will work through those we love to dilute our spiritual strength and to melt and mold us into his own image. Satan works on you, against you, in you and through you, depending on whether you are the tempter, temptress or the tempted. How important this information is for our children who are being raised in this sin sick world! They must be equipped and empowered with spiritual knowledge if they are going to be successful in their Christian walk! If we are going to be successful in our Christian walk, we need to be equipped and empowered with more spiritual knowledge as well.

"Lord, please help us to see that victory is
not by our power nor by our might, but by

> your Spirit! Destroy every yoke and remove every burden that we bear in the areas of pride and self-reliance. Help us to walk away from, turn our backs on the bribes, the positions and the power that this world can offer, and bless us and anoint us to find our contentment in you, in Jesus' name we pray, Amen!"

Remember the plights of Nehemiah and Samson. One survived the storm victoriously, and the other was defeated. We can pass the test with the help of God. The succumbing of the will is a process that must be understood and dealt with by each and every one of us. By no stretch of the imagination should we ever say "we have arrived" as long as our feet are planted on this earth. We should strive to live this life out by the power of the Holy Spirit. Where are we in our battle with temptations? Are we allowing someone, someplace or something to break our will? If so, flee from that person, place or thing as fast as possible to avoid falling prey to the Sixth Step in a temptation, "The Surrendering of the Will".

Chapter Seven
Step 6: The Surrendering of the Will

The sixth step common to temptation is *the surrendering of the will.* "But every man is tempted, when he is drawn away of his own lusts, and enticed. *Then when lust hath conceived,...*" (James 1:14:15). The conception of lusts births *the surrendering of the will* to satan. Webster's definition of *surrender* is "to relinquish possession or control of to another as a result of demand or compulsion; to give up in favor of another; to give over or resign (oneself) to something". This definition is right on track because in each temptation, we have the choice to either retain control of our will or turn it over to another. Satan's overall goal and objective in temptation is to cause us through some medium (people, places, things or events) of the world system (the lusts of the eyes, the lusts of the flesh or the pride of life) to surrender, to submit and to abandon our will to him, in order to break our alliance with God.

Proverbs 23:26 declares, "My son, give me thine heart, and let thine eyes observe my ways." There are several critical points from this text of Scripture that we should highlight and extract for closer examination:

1) The surrendering of the heart to our Father God is the most critical step in the Christian walk. Failure to do so could result in yielding our heart and entire being to someone or something else.
2) The surrendering of the heart to God is the act of our will by choice, and not force. God will never force us to give ourselves to Him. God will never make us do any-

thing; however, He can allow us to become so miserable that we wish we would have yielded ourselves to Him in the first place.

3) The surrendering of the heart is based on an experiential knowledge of the loving, caring relationship that a son has with his father. Satan will attempt to imitate God's love and care, but it is merely an act to deceive us. We can readily distinguish the love of God as it flows out of the Holy Spirit for the purpose of edifying us and glorifying God. Satan will attempt to falsify and misrepresent God's love and care by sending wolves dressed in sheep's clothing, so beware.
4) The surrendering of the heart is greatly impacted by the observance of the eyes. Whatever the eyes behold affects every beat and response of the heart. Lamentations 3:51 declares, "Mine eye affecteth mine heart...", revealing to us the positive or negative relationship between our eyes and our heart.
5) The surrendering of the heart produces either fleshly or spiritual ways. When we surrender our heart to Christ, we see Him, that which pertains to Him, and so we observe and adopt His ways. Alternatively, when we surrender our heart to satan, we see his ways and follow in his steps.

To whom will you yield your heart? To whom will you look and listen? "My sheep hear my voice, and I know them, and they follow me" (John 10:27). Knowing the voice of Jesus is critical to our Christian walk. Even with sincerity of heart, we will surely stumble if we are unable to distinguish the leading of the Spirit from the tug of satan. Many are deceived by spirits that look, feel, taste, smell and sound similar to what they *think* is pure in Spirit. We can get in trouble going by what we *think* is right. The attack of the enemy is sometimes a subtle force that chips away the resolve of the believer. Satan's plea intentionally mimics God. Always remember that satan not only knows the Scriptures, but that he was also cast down from heaven. Oh yes! Satan knows exactly how to manufacture and manipulate the *appearance* of godliness because he once sat in high heavenly places; thus, he is the *greatest* deceiver! Satan uses the same words, "My son, (daughter) give me thine heart", as he attempts to ignite within us a charge to yield to him and "flesh out" on someone or in some situation. Our hearts determine our response to life and its demands. It would stand to reason then that a heart surrendered to Christ responds to life's circumstances in a godly way, and a heart surrendered to satan responds in a fleshly way. Satan must capture our hearts to get to the pulse of our response system if he intends to resurrect and reestablish certain patterns of behavior in our lives issuing from the old man, who walks contrary to the Christian way. In Mark 7:21-23, the Lord Jesus taught the following:

Verse 21: "For from within, *out of the heart* of men, proceed evil thoughts (and then evil acts), adulteries, fornications, murders,

Verse 22: Thefts, covetousness, wickedness, deceit, lasciviousness, an evil eye, blasphemy, pride, foolishness:

Verse 23: All these evil things come from within, and defile the man".

From this Scripture, we can see the importance of surrendering our hearts on a daily basis to our Heavenly Father to ensure we do not give place to the enemy.

By now, we should clearly see the grand scheme of satan's plot in Genesis 3. What was the serpent's overall goal and objective in the Garden of Eden? The serpent's approach and determination was to seize the will of Eve and Adam who embodied all mankind. God's commandment was given indirectly to Eve, so satan's intent was to place a demand on her will that would cause her to completely surrender to him her heart, her life, her resources, her mind, her emotions and her body. The serpent knew that if he could persuade Eve to surrender her will to him, then he would seize Adam's will as well and effectively separate all mankind from the person, presence, provisions, providence and power of God. We are now keenly aware of satan's cycle of temptation. Examine the steps that led to the fall. Review and note the first five steps; the sixth step is newly introduced in this Chapter, and a preview of the final two steps is listed also:

Step 1: Satan first ***stimulates Eve's senses***;

Step 2: Satan ***sows seeds of thought into Eve's mind***;

Step 3: Satan influences and ***stirs the creativity of Eve's imagination***;

Step 4: Satan attacks Eve's innermost desires and lusts as he ***stirs her emotions***;

Step 5: Satan capitalizes on his successes in each preceding step, and uses the combination to dash a powerful blow against Eve to ***weaken her will***;

Step 6: Satan appeals to Eve's heart , and she sees the serpent, then follows and ***surrenders her will*** to him.

Step 7: Satan rejoices as Eve ***commits the sinful act*** of touching and eating the forbidden fruit;

Step 8: Satan delights in ***the result of Eve's sinful act – spiritual death is imparted***, or what is commonly referred to as "the fall of man" has stunned the universe!

In Chapter 5, we studied the Garden of Eden as the "scene of the crime"—the place where we find forensic evidence of satan's fingerprints, his voice recorded and his footprints made. Genesis 3 sprang the cycle of satan's eight deadly steps in temptation into motion, and it has spun out of control ever since the day man was separated from God. No one is exempt from temptation or sin. "But every man is tempted,..." (James 1:14). "For all have sinned, and come short of the glory of God" (Rom. 3:23). The Spirit of God is now moving in us to expose satan's methods so we can be prepared to fight the battle and stand on our feet to shout the victory! Have you ever felt defeated or taken a fall? Perhaps so, when you tried to fight the battle on your own. Must you continue to fall? Absolutely not! Remember the Biblical instructions in Chapter One? "Put on the whole armour of God, that ye may be able to stand against the wiles of the devil" (Eph. 6:11). We are learning how to stand in the face of the enemy. When our will is weak, satan goes in for the kill. Without the *surrendering of the will* to satan, sin can *not* take place. Conversely, our will fully committed and surrendered to Christ can *not* sin. Adam and Eve surrendered their wills to the serpent, and the consequence of their actions handed over to the enemy the will of all mankind. The serpent, satan, accomplished his initial goal, to capture man's organ of decision. With that feat, satan gained access and the ability to influence man's thoughts, imagination, reasoning, memory bank, feelings, desires, affections and will. Since that fateful day in the Garden, man has chosen to do what he deems right in his own eyes!

Romans 6:16 proclaims, "Know ye not, that to whom ye yield yourselves servants to obey, his servants ye are to whom ye obey; whether of sin unto death, or of obedience unto righteousness?" The will of man is now under the auspices of satan, tainted with sin and corruption. Man must now struggle to the point of absolute, total failure to do that which is right in the eyes of God. Paul was led to summarize the condition of the will of man as such in Romans 7:15, 19, "For that which I do I allow not: for what I would, that do I not; but what I hate, that do I" (v.15). "For the good that I would, I do not: but the evil which I would not, that I do" (v.19). The fall of man programmed and conditioned man's will to battle with serving God. The fall of man initialized the propensity of man to serve satan. Why do we have difficulty discerning truth from error? Because we have an inherent nature to surrender our wills to satan, the author of confusion. Similarly, the fall of man has forced man to battle on the opposing side of righteousness and the Spirit. We do not want to represent unrighteousness and the flesh, yet we find ourselves uniformed and suited to volley on their teams. The influence of satan finds us parsing Scripture, arguing over what constitutes holy and that which is sinful. The fall of man has affected man's will in decision making over crucial issues in life, in our cultures, communities and our worlds. Man has since clashed and debated over topics centered around abortion, sex changes, homosexuality, premarital sex, euthanasia, genetic embryonic stem cell research and cloning, political correctness, capital punishment, polygamy, pornography, truth and justice, spiritual, mental and physical adultery, etc. Man's debilitated will has empowered satan's plans and purposes to be revealed and executed in the earth. When we read and hear about adults abusing children, when we see and hear about the corruptness of politicians, when we experience and hear about the rise and fall of our church leaders, when we read the newspapers and hear on the radio about the double agents caught in the act of espionage and treason, when we see and hear television reports about mothers killing their babies, when we read about the innocent dying at the hands of some maniac, when we encounter or read about bomb explosions killing harmless people, then we know that satan is at work manifesting himself in the earth through the wills of mankind.

Please note that if we surrender our wills to satan, he can and will capture our entire being and regulate our worlds. Satan can heavily influence us, if not completely control us, to act out his will in our daily activities. Watch out for the trap! "And that they may recover themselves out of the snare of the devil, who are taken captive by him at his will" (II Tim. 2:26). This Scripture teaches us that satan has a will, and that he has power to act out his will against us because he has temporarily ensnared us through some form of temptation. We must not overlook the fact that the devil, with his limited power, is going to use it against us to the utmost! Satan is going to exercise whatever power he may have against us to trap and destroy us, until we, by the grace of God, come to the knowledge of the truth about the power of the cross, destroying satanic power against the believer! The Bible admonishes us in II Corinthians 2:11 that we should not be ignorant of satan's devices. He uses people, places, things and events to strategize against us to abduct our wills. We must learn how to perceive when satan is at work conniving, deceiving and cheating to exploit our wills! As the watchman on guard duty, we must be on a continual lookout for enemy forces on the horizon! As an air traffic controller in the tower, we must keep a close watch on our radar monitors to ensure that the enemy has not entered our airspace. As a policeman with radar, we must make sure that the enemy is not speeding up and down the interstates of our minds freely. Pull those demons over, ticket and arrest them! Do not allow satan the last dance!

When we find our wills weakened and ready to break down, seek refuge by calling on the name of Jesus for deliverance. Why? Christ is the Answer! The Word of God is all the ammunition we need to stand against satan! "The Lord knoweth how to deliver the godly out of temptations, and to reserve the unjust unto the day of judgment to be punished"! (II Peter 2:9) Hallelujah! Praise God for the victory, and testify of His saving and keeping power!

But what is so significant about our wills? Thank you for asking! As stated above, and worthy of restating, man's will is his organ for decision making and exercising his or her right to select. What we choose to do (or not do) stems from our will. The will is the "helm" on our ships (on our beings) by which we navigate and sail upon the sea of life. Our wills act out or express the chosen desires for the entire person. Our wills are the organs that express our character, whether good or bad, godly or ungodly, mean or kind, short or patient, loving or spiteful, cheerful or depressed, etc. Our emotions merely express how we feel; our minds simply inform us what we are thinking and process such thoughts, but our wills (or volitions) communicate verbally or demonstratively what we want or desire.

THE WILL IS THE MOST INFLUENTIAL COMPONENT IN OUR ENTIRE BEING!! This is why the enemy targets the will through temptation each and every day of our lives. He knows that every day we have to make decisions, because decisions reflect our character and lifestyles. Satan desires to have a say so in the foods we eat (unhealthy foods to ruin our temples). He wants to influence the literature that we read (that which edifies the flesh or soul, but destroys the spirit). He wants to sway our opinions and judgments from righteous thinking to unholy meditations. Satan wants preeminence over directing us to the church where he has his greatest impact. Satan delights in ruining our perspective on the Bride of Christ, for whom Jesus died. He wants to have dominion over the decisions we make—the types of people we meet, date, fellowship with and marry. Satan is not satisfied until he has total possession of our wills so he can determine what drinks we consume (alcoholic beverages which destroy the temple) or what drugs we put in our bodies, whether they are legal or illicit, whether they give us temporary pleasure or cause permanent damage. He craves on defrauding us out of our money, by making us gullible to his scams and rip-offs, e.g., his 10-75% sales, "get-rich-quick" scams, insurance frauds, lemon car sales, charity dupes, etc. He longs to help us formulate attitudes of unforgiveness, bitterness, jealousy, resentment, hatred, anger, pride, competition, unthankfulness, etc. He fans the flames of malice against our loved ones so that he can create dissension in the household between husband and wife, parent and child, brother to brother, sister to sister, aunt or uncle to nephew or niece, etc. He gets excited about sending us to work in a bad mood or causing us to cop a bad disposition with our bosses, coworkers or our work in general.

The influence of satan rallies around thoughts of helplessness, suicide and depression during seasons of financial stress, e.g., a bear market place. Satan severely attacks the lonely and distraught. He whips us to a pulp with his "woe is me" belt when we feel life has dealt us a bad hand, when we are experiencing the loss of a job, a car, a home, a dear family member, or someone we held close as the love of our lives. We sometimes fail to realize how satan perpetuates our feelings of despair, frustration and hopelessness. Satan hears our songs and praises. We sing "My Hope Is Built on Nothing Less Than Jesus Blood and Righteousness ... On Christ the Solid Rock I Stand. All Other Ground is Sinking Sand"! Satan knows when we are merely making musical mimes and going through the motions of the melody with hymnals in hand, genuinely uncommitted to the depths of our utterances! We rejoice and sing "Don't Wait Until the Battle's Over, Shout Now!" on Sunday, and then quickly slip into a state of hopelessness about our unemployment on Monday. When our children's change in behavior appears impossible or a transformation in our spouse's mental, physical, drug and alcohol abuse seems unfathomable, satan keeps piling it on. Oh yes! He wants to be a part of and manage dictatorially our every waking and sleeping moment. He desires to make every day a challenge, a formidable task, a question as to whether or not life is worth living at all! Lord, *please* help us to see beyond the veil!!

In Chapter Four, we studied satan's influence on *the creativity of the imagination.* Let's revisit the Book of Isaiah to further examine the rise and fall of Lucifer, the son of the morning. The Spirit of God reveals how and why Lucifer fell. Lucifer's heart was full of pride, and he was receiving counsel within himself from himself. Self was out of control and started formulating thoughts and desires and releasing strength through its own words that led to his fall. When self is in control, it always stresses itself through the words "I Will". These are the two most dangerous words in heaven and in earth when used outside the context of the name of Jesus. Lucifer flooded his thoughts, his desires, his imagination, his reasoning, his memory bank and his heart with those words until it created within him a "self induced", "self generated" and "self motivated" monster. After the fall of man, this beast became known as the "flesh". Isaiah 14:12-15 reads as follows:

Verse 12: How art thou fallen from heaven, O Lucifer, son of the morning! How art thou cut down to the ground, which didst weaken the nations!

Verse 13: For thou hast said in thine heart, I will ascend into heaven, I will exalt my throne above the stars of God: I will sit also upon the mount of the congregation, in the sides of the north:

Verse 14: I will ascend above the heights of the clouds; I will be like the most High.

Verse 15: Yet thou shalt be brought down to hell, to the sides of the pit.

In this passage, Lucifer manifested self will against the will of God. Notice what he said in verse 13, "I will ascend into heaven" (self will), "I will exalt my throne above the stars of God" (self exaltation) and "I will sit also upon the mount of the congregation, in the sides of the north" (self enthronement). Then in verse 14, he continues his determined mental and emotional quest by thinking and speaking, "I will ascend above the heights of the clouds" (self ascension) and "I will be like the most High" (self deification). Lucifer had literally *lost his mind*! He had purposed in his heart to dethrone God and become "god" in God's place. He actually believed what he said and tried to will them into existence, forgetting all about the fact that the will of the creature is <u>*always*</u> subject to the will of the Creator! Hallelujah! Lucifer did not create God, but God created Lucifer! Lucifer did not will God into existence, God willed Lucifer into existence. God created Lucifer to service the most High God! Lucifer's thinking became warped!! Had he sat out in the sun entirely too long? He was obviously delusional, clearly unwell. Perhaps someone or something had hit him in the head! He became self righteous and began justifying himself to himself, lifting up himself before himself, worshipping and offering himself unto himself. His will expressed the desires and the intent of his heart in heaven. Upon being cast down and out of heaven, or as Jesus said in Luke 10:18, "And he said unto them, I beheld Satan as lightning fall from heaven", Lucifer, now turned satan, brought with him the nature that had betrayed him.

In the Garden of Eden, satan's will found expression through the serpent's temptation. The fall of man ensued, and the cycle of temptation and sin ushered in the reproduction of satan's will and his selfish, fleshly nature into all mankind. Prior to his entrance into the Garden, and subsequent to the fall of mankind, the term "flesh" was not found in the earth. It was after the fall that the will of the flesh, the will of self, the will of satan, and the will of the world found a door or a portal through sin in which to walk into the hearts and lives of mankind. When man was cast out of the Garden, his will—the power to choose and the ability to select the things of God went out of the Garden as well. The potential of receiving and assimilating the nature and character of God ceased to exist. Man's will could now only produce fleshly, sensual results.

In Genesis 4:1-15, we find the story of Cain and Abel. Cain and Abel are brothers who hold two very different jobs. Cain is a groundskeeper and Abel is a shepherd. The tension begins when the two brothers offer sacrifices to God. The Lord respects Abel's sheep offering (v.4). Cain offers God the "fruit of the ground" (v.3), and the Lord disrespects his sacrifice (v.5). Cain is clearly disturbed by the rejection, and his jealousy gets the best of him. Cain is tempted of satan, and eventually *surrenders his will* to him. Cain's heart is in the wrong place, so we see the manifestation of his untamed, selfish will when he chooses to murder Abel. We learn from

Cain's transgression that sin is a byproduct of surrendering the will to satan. We all see things that happen to other people who we deem less worthy of the blessing. Beware! Allowing satan an opening through the receptors of our senses triggers the first step in the process of temptation. Once he gains access (Step One), satan will implant an unhealthy seed of thought in the mind (Step Two). The next thing we know, we're thinking of ways to "wipe out" the other person from the pictures of our imagination (Step Three), and our satan influenced imagination stirs up the jealousy and lusts of our emotions (Step Four). The combination of all these steps lean on our will until it is weakened (Step Five), and then we completely surrender our will to satan (Step Six), and the sinful act is committed (Step Seven). We will later examine the result, consequences and wages of sin, i.e., spiritual death (Step Eight). Don't allow satan the opening! Remember "the domino effect"? Once satan tips his first step in a temptation, the pressure rapidly begins to snowball against our will. Nip satan's game in the bud early on! Find the key to victory in the Word of God. Pray and trust God for complete deliverance. Keep the mind of Christ for a blessed daily walk in Him!

In Genesis 6:3-7, Jehovah summarized the condition of man's will as being "wicked". Remember, the will reveals the sum total of our character and personality, our root and our fruit, our attitudes and our actions. Therefore, Jehovah called mankind "wicked", and it was His will to destroy everything He had created from off the face of the earth. Parents? Can you relate? You gave birth to your children. You fed them when they were hungry. You provided clothing for them when they were naked. You loved and cared for them as they needed attention, and then those very same offspring rise up to spite you! My Lord! Have you ever found yourself so disgusted with the actions of your children that you gave serious thought to dismissing them from their present condition on earth? Be honest! Help us to hold out Lord! God found himself in that grievous position. In Genesis 6:11-13, God said to Noah:

Verse 11 The earth also was corrupt before God, and the earth was filled with violence.

Verse 12: And God looked upon the earth, and, behold, it was corrupt; for all flesh had corrupted his way upon the earth.

Verse 13: And God said unto Noah, The end of all flesh is come before me; for the earth is filled with violence through them; and, behold, I will destroy them with the earth.

God was fed up with man yielding his will to the flesh (satan). He was sick and tired of the irreverent will of mankind disgracing the earth! Do you ever wonder if God is saying the same thing to us today?

In Genesis 11:1-9, we find another instance of God's wrath on mankind at the Tower of Babel. When the children of men decided to build a city and a tower to reach to heaven for their own glory, they were confounded when the Lord said, "Behold, the people is one, and they have all one language; and this they begin to do: and now nothing will be restrained from them, which they have imagined to do" (v.6). Jehovah had to nix their unseemly behavior. He descended into the earth, and confounded their language. The confusion was so great, that the construction ended, the people scattered, and the place was called Babel. We have much to learn from this passage of Scripture. When we surrender our wills to our imaginations, we run the risk of making a mockery of our selfish creativeness and losing fellowship with God and those most important to our stability.

Has God ever called you to do anything, and you tried to "help Him out" a little bit? No doubt, we could swap stories all day on how our wills clash with the divine will of God! Let's be encouraged because this "battle of the wills" has been fought since the beginning. In Genesis 12, Jehovah made a covenant with Abram. God promised to show Abram a new land and to bless his seed. When food got scarce, Abram forsook the promised land and went to Egypt. This was his first mistake! Abram had an attractive wife named Sarai. He was afraid he might be killed in Egypt because others would covet her. Abram thought he would exercise his own will over the will of God. He told Sarai to tell the people in Egypt that she was his sister instead of his wife—just a self preserving "little white lie". This was his second mistake! He revealed once again the instability and the autonomy of his human will at work against the will of God. Abram reasoned his way into a bind with God. He reasoned that his actions were necessary for survival, and further rationalized that survival was a requirement to fulfill God's covenant! Can't you hear Abram pondering the following to himself: "How can all the families of the earth be blessed through me if I starve and die? If I should go to where the food is, wouldn't I do well to protect myself from being destroyed over some foolishness down in Egypt? After all. God needs me to fulfill His covenant." And we say to Brother Abram, "Please and no thank you! God can handle it!" Whether Abram or a Twenty-first century believer, <u>*watch it*</u>! God will <u>*never*</u> require you to sin in order to promote you in His Kingdom. God can NOT sin or provoke such temptation. Guess who can? Satan!! Abram relinquished his will to the fear of his circumstances and conceived and contrived his own plan of how to cope with his issues at hand. Ultimately, he relinquished his will to the enemy, because fear is not of God and neither is that lying spirit that he manifested.

In Genesis 16, Sarai exercises her will by playing the "dating game" with her husband, Abram, and her Egyptian handmaid, Hagar. Sarai was barren, so she took matters into her own hands, and decided to "help God out" by offering Hagar to Abram to assist in making good on the covenant since she (Sarai) wasn't able to procreate quickly enough for her own comfort. Hagar did conceive, and Abram named his son Ishmael. According to the angel of the Lord, "... he will be a wild man; his hand will be against every man, and every man's hand against him; and he shall dwell in the presence of all his brethren" (v.12). Sarai lived to regret her hasty mistake. An entire nation suffers because she did not wait on the will of God.

In Genesis 19, the men of Sodom exposed the carnality and the lewdness in their hearts when they conceived in their hearts and willed in their minds to know the men who were invited to tarry in Lot's house for the night. The results of such behavior resulted in total destruction of the city. Why? Because the will of man demonstrated the wickedness abounding in the heart of man. Once again, the wickedness conceived in the heart of man was a stench in the nostrils of Jehovah, showing that man's will had resigned itself to follow satan's plans.

Our wills stand between two worlds, the spiritual and the natural. Every decision we make is formed by the will and is either influenced by the Spirit of God and the Word of God or by satan, self, the world and the flesh. Our decisions and behavior reveal whether we are filled with the Spirit and the Word, emptied of ourselves, or filled with the flesh and ourselves. Galatians 5:19-23 captures the manifestations of our wills when stimulated and animated by the Holy Spirit or satan. Habitual acts are formed through the decision making branch called the will. Executive orders are carried out by the will. Judicial statements are spoken through the unction of the will. Therefore, whoever is in control of the surrendered will wins the battle!

Let it be known that it is God's will for us to be shaped and conformed into the image of Christ! (Rom. 8:29) However, satan has another plan in mind. He wants our wills passive and inactive to perform the will of God, and active to execute his satanic will. Because satan had and has a desire to be like God, he desires us to worship him, behold him, think, speak and behave as he does. Satan wants us. He influences and seeks to direct our wills to respond to other persons, places or things as if he, himself, were so engaged in the act. When we adhere to satan and rebel against God, it appears as if we are rendering an eternal "no" to the will of God and an abiding "yes" to satan. Is this your choice? Have you been operating in the dark, thinking you were accepting God's will, only to be fulfilling the will of the enemy? Is satan hiding behind the choices you make? He did it to Peter in Matthew 16:22-23. Is he setting you up and then leaving you to accept the consequences? He did it to Judas in Matthew 27:3-5. Far too many times have we allowed this rascal to set us up, not knowing that we would be left all alone to bear the brunt of the fall.

Sooner or later, we all must come to the realization that our wills should belong to God and that He, and He alone, is the safety net for our entire being. We need to understand the importance of godly counsel in every decision we make. We can pay up front by taking our time before making decisions, or pay later because we chose not to count the cost. Which will it be for you, pleasure or pain? ... feast or famine? ... sunshine or rain? ... health or wealth? ... sickness or poverty? Please surrender your will to God and at all cost, avoid the will of the enemy to avoid falling into the clutches of Step Eight, "The Sinful Act Committed".

EXTERNAL ACTS MANIFESTED

Chapter Eight
Step 7: The Sinful Act Committed

The seventh step common to temptation is *the sinful act committed*. "Then when lust hath conceived, *it bringeth forth sin*..." (James 1:15). Until now, we have focused on the *internal* course of satan's temptations. We will now focus on what happens *externally*:

1. *after* our senses (step 1) provide an allowance for satan to sow a corrupt seed of thought into our mind (step 2);
2. *after* our imagination is overcome by the influence of satan (step 3);
3. *after* our inner lusts and desires become emotionally stirred up (step 4); and
4. *after* our will is weakened (step 5) and surrendered (step 6) to satan.

When we allow satan to take control, his first six steps in temptation go unchecked, unbridled and unrebuked. *After* we yield to all of these *internal* blows of the enemy, the result of his attack manifests itself *externally* in the form of "sin" (step 7). Sin relates to the act, and not to the nature (or flesh); however, in order to commit sin, we must operate out of the sinful fleshly nature. Sin can be committed in word (Matt. 5:33-37), thought (Matt. 5:27-30) or deed (Matt. 5:31-32). In Chapter Three, we learned that sin can be conceived and committed in and through our thought life. It does not stop there, however! Did you know that sin can be conceived and uttered through the words sown and retained in our hearts? Oh yes! The Word says "In transgressing and lying against the Lord, and departing away from God, speaking oppression and revolt, conceiving and uttering from the heart words of falsehood (Isaiah 59:13). In the previous chapter, we opened up the Word of God and placed Proverbs 23:26 under the magnifying scope to clearly see the connection between the heart and the will. We discovered that a heart committed to Christ surrenders to the will of God, and a heart committed to satan surrenders its will to temptation and sin. Have you ever heard the following popular clichés: "*If it's in you, it's coming out* or *Show me your true colors*?" This jargon applied to our study on temptation is interpreted "How *soon* will your words and deeds reveal the contents of your heart?" The Word of God speaks on the outward manifestation of the conceptions of our heart:

> "O generation of vipers, how can ye, being evil, speak good things? for out of the abundance of the heart the mouth speaketh" (Matt. 12:34).
>
> "A good man out of the good treasure of his heart bringeth forth that which is good; and an evil man out of the evil treasure of his heart bringeth forth that which is evil: for of the abundance of the heart his mouth speaketh" (Luke 6:45).

Where is your heart today? The key to your salvation lies in the answer to that question! You can NOT and will NOT be defeated by satan's temptations with a fully committed heart to Jesus! There it is! Total commitment to Christ is the Answer! Only in Him can we stand victoriously against the attack of the enemy! Praise God in all His glory, Hallelujah! We must know and be encouraged by the fact that satan shrieks from the believer who is perfectly armed with the Word of God. Perfectly armed? In boot camp, trainees are taught that their weapons are a part of them. They must know their weapons meticulously and intimately. In order to prevail against the enemy, the drill sergeant screams in the face of the young private the importance of cleaning his weapon, how to dismantle and reassemble it, how to load ammunition, and how to perfectly arm himself with that weapon to save his life in the heat of battle. ONLY a perfectly armed soldier survives. When the seasoned soldier finds himself in the heat of the battlefield, with enemy fire coming from every direction, his survival depends on those boot camp survival tactics that seemed so remote from reality at the time. Christians are in an active campaign against satan. Are you perfectly armed today? Is your Bible collecting dust from Sunday to Sunday? Do you know that the Book of Galatians immediately follows II Corinthians, or do you need to check the Table of Contents each time you search the Scriptures? Do you study the Word? How meticulous and intimate are you with the Word? Oh this is it! This key to your salvation is what the demons are fussing and cursing about this instant because you are reading this book to expose their only true fear — God and His Word! Believe it, and then DO what the Word says! A perfectly armed believer not only reads, but also studies, meditates, internalizes and utilizes the Word of God! Prepare your heart for victory! Yield to Christ and surrender your will to Him, and He will keep you from falling. Enjoy His protection, and beat the adversary down with the mighty Sword of the Spirit! "Thy word have I hid in mine heart, that I might not sin against thee" (Psalms 119:11).

In addition to sin wreaking havoc in our thoughts and the utterances of our heart, it is committed and manifested through our deeds or works. Out of our sinful nature called "the flesh" or the "old man", we commit sinful acts. "That which is born of the flesh is flesh;..." (John 3:6). "...for whatsoever a man soweth, that he shall also reap. For he that soweth to his flesh shall of the flesh reap corruption" (Gal. 6:7,8). These Scriptures reveal the principle that the sinful nature of the flesh produces sinful acts continually. The Lord Jesus, himself, taught us that the act is consistent with the nature, i.e., the fruit on the tree is consistent with the root of the tree. "Even so every good tree bringeth forth good fruit; but a corrupt tree bringeth forth evil fruit. A good tree cannot bring forth evil fruit, neither can a corrupt tree bring forth good fruit" (Matt. 7:17-18). The "Wisdom Writer" declared "the root of the righteous yieldeth the fruit" (Prov. 12:12), and we find this Word remarkably prophetic and parallel to the spoken word of the Master in Matthew 7:17-18.

The Bible says "What? know ye not that your body is the temple of the Holy Ghost which is in you, which ye have of God, and ye are not your own?" (I Cor. 6:19) Excuse me? Certainly. We belong to God? Indeed. We are not our own? *Absolutely* NOT! Well then, <u>*who*</u> rules our bodies or temples? "... choose you this day whom ye will serve... (Joshua 24:15). We have the will to choose whether we dwell in darkness or light. Satan can not operate in the light. He rules the kingdom of darkness. God and His Word are beacons of light. The Psalmist David declares, "Thy Word is a lamp unto my feet, and a light unto my path" (Psalms 119:105). When we are faced with temptation, we can trump the darkness with the light of victory found in God's Word! There is protection and safety in a temple illuminated by Christ. Are you familiar with a circuit breaker?

It is a powerful unit that controls the power in a building. There are breaker switches that can be turned to the *on* or *off* positions. When the switches are flipped *on*, we enjoy floods of light and the convenience of functioning equipment and useful appliances. When the switches are flipped to the *off* position, then there is darkness, silence and inactivity from everything governed by that switch. Think of this illustration in a spiritual sense, relating to God and satan. God represents light or the *on* position. Satan hates brilliance and harmony, so he seeks to control every switch in our temple by turning them to the *off* position where dysfunctional darkness, weakness and sin abide. He has a field day watching us stumble around in confused darkness. Avoid satan's hand on the controls of your temple! Rebuke him! Remind him that you belong to God and strive daily to walk in the light! Even in the midst of your storm, when sunshine is only a trace of a silver lining hidden behind the clouds, seek the light for refuge and salvation. According to His Word, God will deliver! "He that dwelleth in the secret place of the most High shall abide under the shadow of the Almighty" (Psalms 91:1). There can be no shadow without the presence of light! We do not have to fall when we have the power of God's glory within! Do you believe it? Then, stake your position in the light. Be vigilant! Guard your temple from the onslaught of the enemy, and stay *on* for God! Isn't it good to know that we have an outlet in Christ for a way of escape from sin? Hallelujah!

We must know how temptations operate in order to stop the process. If we do not understand the intricate details of satan's attack, how then can we effectively pray for those operations to cease? We are studying both the internal and external manifestations of temptation with all diligence so we can "nip them in the bud" internally before the act of sin is committed externally. Satan can not smoothly orchestrate his cycle of temptation without breaking our spiritual connection to God. Should we allow the enemy the slightest opening (through our senses), he steps right in to take control of our soul and body. Satan takes on the role of the smooth operator. He begins to selectively flip each internal switch of our soul to govern our minds (reasoning, knowledge, understanding, wisdom), imagination (resident designer/interior decorator), emotions (desires, feelings, affections) and our will (organ of choice and decision making). Satan then externally effects change in our bodies (corporately) or within the members of our bodies (individually). In other words, in order for satan, sin, the flesh, self or the world to cause us to fall into a temptation, they must challenge and change the way we think, imagine, feel and desire God or the things of God. Satan tempts us to question the validity of God's Word and the benefits of walking, talking and maintaining a healthy godly image. Temptation comes to buckle our resolve to attend church services, fellowship with the saints, worship God in Spirit and in truth and read and study the Bible daily. The enemy sows seeds of doubt into our minds about our decisions, e.g., singing gospel music without compromising it for a larger contract in the secular world or choosing sermons that tickle ears without jarring tears. Beware of the enemy's tactics.

Once sin is committed, the resolve to run from temptation, to turn away from watching alluring television shows is gone! The ability to avoid drinking alcoholic beverages, to avoid premarital sex, to speak the truth without telling a little white lie has dissolved. The power to stop slandering or gossiping about our brother or sister, to avoid attending happy hour, to stay at home on Friday and Saturday night instead of going out partying or dancing is non-existent.

The grace to stop smoking marijuana, to stop snorting cocaine, to end that extramarital relationship, to terminate that relationship with a needle, to change the lifestyle of homosexuality has been terminated. The energy to make a conscious effort to make it to work on time, to stop squandering money, to discontinue misusing and abusing people and their resources, is *gone with the wind* when satan controls the soul! Switch by switch, (mind, imagination, emotion and will) satan changes the character from light to darkness, and the expressions of the individual from spiritual to fleshly, until finally they no longer are conformed into the image of Christ, but into the image of himself. The Bible teaches us in Romans 6:6, "that our old man is crucified with Him". In order for the enemy to operate, he must revitalize the "old man" (the crucified soul, the old self, the old mind, will, and emotions) if he is to advance his kingdom through us and if he is going to trap us into walking according to our flesh. When he flips the internal switches of our renewed human soul from the *on* position towards God to the *off* position towards himself, what he is actually doing is turning the switches to the *on* position towards the flesh, sending power to it and resurrecting it from the "crucified" or "dead" state to a "revivified" or "live" state for his unholy service. Once the internal levers of our human "circuit breakers" have been flipped, and darkness (where and how satan operates) or the lack of God's insight (knowledge, understanding and wisdom) has dominion, then the body partakes or becomes involved in the sinister act conceived—sin. Romans 6:6 labels the body controlled by sin or the sin nature, especially in a temptation, as the "body of sin". The body reacts as a puppet to the command and control of satan, sin, self, the flesh and the world system. The "body of sin" must be liberated from the bondage of satan's dominion and temptation's pull. It is therefore the "body of sin" that must experience freedom in order to practice righteousness in the face of lawlessness, and reformulate habits and destructive lifestyles while under the tyranny of sin. Jesus taught in Mark 4:22, "For there is nothing hid, which shall not be manifested; neither was any thing kept secret, but that it should come abroad." We are again reminded that our works broadcast to all a display of the motives and intents of our heart. "Ye shall know them by their fruits" (Matt. 7:16).

We now have a blueprint on sin and the temptations of satan. We see the master plan of the enemy—how he builds and destroys us, both figuratively and literally. What a powerful lesson for us to learn, to grasp and to apply, that we can trace the actions of the flesh and self back to the senses, the thoughts, the desires, the imagination, the environment, the associations and the influences in the life of an individual. We can rebuild the circumstances in our lives in much the same way an architect or construction crew is tasked to redesign and rebuild houses and great skyscrapers that have been devastated by a storm. The experts must first assess the damage and clean up. Then an investigative/planning process begins. A study of logistics must be conducted in order to examine or scrutinize any construction flaws in the original structure, and then new input is required to develop a renewed master plan or blueprint of the building. Our buildings (bodies) encounter such degenerative and rebuilding processes. We are now keenly aware that the actions of the body are directly linked to the heart, and that our ways reflect the object of our commitment. Is the object of your heart God or satan? Loving God with all our heart and clinging to His Word will produce godly actions. Of course, satan is busy vying for our affection—surrendering the will to his temptations will surely produce sin. We can determine why "we do the things we do" by tracing whose steps we choose to follow. We are being made aware of the spiritual source of our outward activities. Sin is the outward result of inwardly surrendering to satan's temptations. "For the wages of sin is death, but the gift of God is eternal life" (Rom. 6:23).

The United States of America and the world were severely impacted by the catastrophic events of September 11, 2001. The attacks against the United States were feverishly planned, and to a great extent, ferociously executed. Let's consider the act of terrorism and the making of a terrorist. According to Webster, terrorism is "the systematic use of terror especially as a means of coercion [force]". There is no question that the events of September 11, 2001 can be characterized as a systematic, well orchestrated operation to destroy lives and cause fear in the hearts of people by coercive, forceful intimidation. Did planning of the event just happen overnight? No, of course not! Some of the participants in the act were willing to die for their cause, which suggests a psychological commitment of the mind as well as the physical commitment of the body. A cycle of operant conditioning of the mind to achieve a physical, visceral propensity toward human destruction must fully run its course before a terrorist act is completed. WHAT? In short, some person, place, thing, event or spirit must heavily influence an individual to participate in a plan designed to take his own life, or the life (lives) of another.

No sane (or arguably insane) person wakes up in the morning, washes his face, brushes his teeth, sits down for breakfast, reads the newspaper, sips orange juice and coffee, swallows a bagel, makes a couple of calls, and then goes out to destroy himself and thousands of others without a programmed brain and agenda. Whose program and agenda would perpetrate such an act of violence? The true perpetrator is neither Middle Eastern, European, Asian, African, American, etc. This warfare is spiritual! "For we wrestle not against flesh and blood, but against principalities, against powers, against the rulers of the darkness of this world, against spiritual wickedness in high places" (Eph. 6:12). The character we need to wrestle down and stop dead in his tracks is not hiding out in a mountain cave! The enemy with whom we are presently engaged in battle is having a field day attacking homes, churches, institutions of higher learning and finance, businesses and governments all over this world!

The destructive god of this world is satan, and we have studied his tactics on every page of this book! If ever there were a time to recognize the methods and operations of temptation, it is NOW. He is the programmer of the suicide bomber and the terrorist. He is the master trainer! Satan knows that if he can tempt the people on one side of the world or street to take a look (senses) at those on the other side of the world or street, then he can get an opening to sow seeds of thought into the minds to whip up bizarre schemes of destruction in the imaginations to promulgate superiority, inferiority, inequity, jealousy, covetousness, greed, etc! After he pierces the senses and gets into the mind and imagination, he delights in promoting hatred, an emotion of the flesh and soul, and a fruit from the fleshly tree. When hatred is stirred up, it gives birth to the will deciding to comply with this act. Once the heart is committed to satan, and the will is completely surrendered, then the result is SIN.

September 11, 2001 is cited as the worst attack ever on American soil and in the history of America, an infamous date when thousands of innocent lives were lost due to the hatred in the heart of a man, organization or state against another. Internal hatred exploded into the external loss of lives, buildings, resources, pride, and security. Bottom line, sow the seed of hatred, reap the manifestation in whatever form designed in the mind of the hater! These are the steps that satan puts into operation to cause someone, especially believers, to fall prey and yield themselves to his destructive plans. Even now, after the airplane attacks on the World Trade Center, the Pentagon, and unrealized targets, we are being challenged to allow the seed of unforgiveness to take root in our hearts. Don't you hear the voice of satan saying:

> "How can you forgive someone who would take innocent lives? How can you merely turn your back on someone who has killed innocent parents and children, husbands and wives, employers and employees, firemen and policemen? How can you find within your heart to forgive when you hurt so badly, have shed so many tears and felt so many unwarranted fears? How can you accept the fact that households are so greatly impacted, holidays for families forever marred, children permanently severed from the warmth and love of their parents?"

How? That dastardly devil is playing on both sides of the court! He is using them against us and when he is charged with the fault, he scurries to the other side of the line to use us against them. Please be careful to watch and pray! Retaliation, which belongs to God, can be just as, if not more deadly, than the original offense. In Judges 11:7, Jephthah experienced great hatred from his own people. He was thrust out of his father's house because he was born of a strange woman. The seed of hatred can manifest itself in multiple ways. History records the pains of slavery, banishment and terrorism. "Dearly beloved, avenge not yourselves, but rather give place unto wrath: for it is written, Vengeance is mine; I will repay, saith the Lord" (Rom. 12:19).

Do you remember Joseph in Genesis 37? Joseph was the favored son of Jacob. He was a gifted visionary or dreamer, and his father honored him with a coat of many colors (v. 3). Joseph's brothers were not feeling any love for their brother. In fact, "they hated him and could not speak peaceably unto him" (v.4). The spirit of hatred teamed with a retaliatory spirit and caused the brothers to steal his coat, cast him into a pit and leave him for dead. Of course, we know how the story ends. While satan meant it for evil, God meant it for good. Joseph's brothers later bowed down to him (Gen. 42:6), a blessed and highly favored governor during the famine in Egypt.

My God, if we ever needed to understand how to discern the activities of the enemy, we surely do right now! We see how jealousy defeated Joseph's brothers. What about envy? When we see or hear about what someone has or is believed to have, we have a human tendency to envy or covet our neighbor's possessions. Remember, that a seed of thought can lead to sin. Jealousy, envy and covetousness often lead to ungodly actions, so we would do well to guard our hearts against jealousy and covetousness toward what we perceive as another's "greener pastures". The unimaginable manifests its ugly head when envy prevails. If we are not careful and prayerful, we will find ourselves moving under the program of satan, planning the demise of or stealing from another. Envy, hate and jealousy can give way to lying, competitive, destructive spirits. Under the influence of satan, we are defeated; "But seek ye first the kingdom of God, and his righteousness; and all these things shall be added unto you" (Matt. 6:33). God has promised those who live a victorious, overcoming Christian life an abundance of blessings, and His rewards are far greater than anything satan can offer!

Temptation that expresses itself externally through the body is our primary focal point in this chapter; however, we must be clear about the commission of sin. It is neither our desire, nor is it Biblical to suggest that sin is only committed externally. The Lord Jesus taught us in Matthew 5:27-32, that there is the possibility of committing sin within before it ever manifests itself without. Paraphrasing, "Whosoever looks with the desire to act, and then executes in their mind the act that they desire, has committed sin in his heart already". Therefore, we must earnestly heed the dictates of the Holy Spirit through the conscience of our human spirit to avoid this type of temptation.

In this phase of temptation, the will switches gears. Where our organ of choice once performed righteous acts, it now executes unrighteous acts, depending on the resident driver or master who we allow to take over the reins of our being. We exercise the will to choose who governs the attitude and the outcome of our condition. The Bible declares in Romans 6:16, "Know ye not, that to whom ye yield yourselves servants to obey, his servants ye are to whom ye obey; whether of sin unto death, or of obedience unto righteousness?" In this case, sin, our former master, according to Romans 6:6, regains the throne of our hearts and lives, and leads us down the broad way and through the wide gate before entering death's door. In this phase of the temptation, the body is reengaged to carry out sin's lusts, the desires of our flesh, another's fleshly desires, satan's desires or the world system's wishes. "...For as ye have yielded your members servants to uncleanness and to iniquity unto iniquity;..." (Rom.6:19). This passage of Scripture indicates that our bodies and bodily parts are under sin's dominion – instruments for satan's use. These same members, which were being used for good, now become rehired, reactivated and revitalized as instruments of unrighteousness employed by sin to accomplish its goals and objectives conceived in the heart. According to Romans 6:6, the once annulled, destroyed or unemployed "body of sin" now finds itself working in the evil economy of the enemy and getting paid for it. Although the enemy does pay, the wages earned are deadly and fatal. Remember, the Scriptures teach us that "… the wages of sin is death…" (Rom. 6:23). Satan is an employer without a benefit package. Work is being performed, but with only temporary satisfaction. Sinful works being performed through fleshly appetites cause us to miss out on the family inheritance (Gal. 5:21). That was Paul's message to the church at Galatia, and the same holds true for us today. If we continue to operate in our flesh, and war against the human spirit and the Holy Spirit, we too may miss out on our future inheritance and the abundant life which is made available to us right now!

When we live by the life of the flesh, we walk in the flesh. When we walk in flesh, we are energized by the flesh and are actually walking in darkness. To walk in darkness is to think, move and respond according to the dictates of the counsel of the enemy or the "inner me" (Rom. 8:5-8). When we are walking in darkness, our human spirit is in bondage, our human soul is under the control of satan and our human body is executing his plan. To allow the influence of the adversary to guide us into darkness is to operate in satan's domain. When we are operating in satan's domain, he is trying to ruin our lives, destroy our testimonies, initiate sinful thoughts, cause us to act in sinful ways and inject us with his diabolical nature to cause spiritual death. But what is spiritual death? What does it mean to walk in spiritual death? This leads us into our final chapter and final step, "Spiritual Death Imparted".

Chapter Nine
Step 8: Spiritual Death Imparted

The eighth and final step common to temptation is *spiritual death imparted.*, "... and sin, when it is finished, *bringeth forth death*" (James 1:15). This final step focuses on the impact of sin on our fellowship with God. Sin separates the human spirit from communion with the Holy Spirit. This grave condition is called *spiritual death*. God's Word declares "For the wages of sin is death; but the gift of God is eternal life through Jesus Christ our Lord" (Romans 6:23). Christ is the giver and sustainer of life. "For in Him we live, and move, and have our being..." (Acts 17:28). When we sin, our lifeline to the Kingdom of Heaven is instantly severed. Sin jeopardizes the placement of our name in the Lamb's book of life! "And there shall in no wise enter into it [heaven] any thing that defileth, neither whatsoever worketh abomination, or maketh a lie: but they which are written in the Lamb's book of life" (Rev. 21:27). Believers, remember that **nothing** threatens to break the stride of our Christian walk quicker than temptation, and *absolutely* **nothing** is more devastating to our salvation than surrendering our will to satan, falling in sin and suffering *spiritual death*!!

In each chapter of this book, we have studied the process of temptation as revealed in James 1, verses 14 and 15. In fact, we have carefully and methodically dissected this inspired Word of God in order to expose satan's eight deadly steps in temptation. Let's review the text once again for emphasis and commitment to memory:

Verse 14: But every man is tempted, ***when*** he is drawn away of his own lust, and enticed.

Verse 15: ***When*** lust hath conceived, it bringeth forth sin: and sin, ***when*** it is finished, bringeth forth death.

Please note that the word ***when*** trisects this passage of Scripture into distinct phases of temptation. The "***when*** factor" is noteworthy because there is profound significance in viewing the processes of temptation and birth under the same scope. In this light, we find that each process is divided into three stages or trimesters, and that both temptation and birth deal with conception, bringing forth life and the finality of death. While natural conception, childbirth and life are destined for physical death, believers should know that the downward spiraling cycle of temptation can be aborted before experiencing the external manifestations of sin and *spiritual death*. How is that possible? The Bible gives us this assurance! "There hath no temptation taken you but such as is common to man: but God is faithful, who will not suffer you to be tempted above that ye are able; but will with the temptation also make a way to escape, that ye may be able to bear it" (I Cor. 10:13). Hallelujah! Now, let's examine the three phases of the "***when*** factor" revealed in James 1, verses 14 and 15, to learn more about our "way to escape":

Temptation Trimester One: "But every man is tempted *when* he is drawn away...". If we believe what this course of study has already exposed about satan's tactics, then we should be confident that we can rebuke the devil to emerge victoriously from this first phase of spiritual warfare.

Temptation Trimester Two: "Then *when* lust hath conceived... " Albeit a greater challenge to achieve balance and recovery from these advanced blows of satan's attack, it is encouraging to know that we can survive spiritually if we resist the enemy and totally lean on and trust God for complete deliverance!

Temptation Trimester Three: "...and sin, *when* it is finished, bringeth forth death." Lord, Help us! We're in trouble with sin! "Three strikes, we're *OUT*" of communion with the Holy Spirit, and the sinful act ushers on a swift and certain *spiritual death*.

From the moment of natural conception, amniotic fluid forms a protective sac around the human embryo and growing fetus. This life sustaining fluid produced by the placenta and fetus allows the developing baby to move inside the womb, and is essential for uniform growth of bones and tissue. Amniotic fluid is the substance or lifeline the baby breathes in and out in order to survive inside the womb. You are probably familiar with amniocentesis—a medical procedure typically administered in the second trimester of pregnancy to reveal the baby's development. By extracting fluid from the mother's amniotic sac, doctors can assess the development of the fetus. However, there are controversial risks associated with the invasive nature of amniocentesis because the procedure requires a needle injection into the womb for extraction of the precious fluid. Both the benefit and risk are found in the injection. The properly administered procedure extracts the life preserving fluid for diagnosis while the botched procedure can be costly. Should the gauge of the needle be too great, inject the womb too frequently or in an instant of misdirection, pierce the baby, a spontaneous abortion is likely to occur. Of course, no expectant mother who desires a full term delivery would consent to a test that would result in certain death. She would be compelled to listen very carefully to her doctor's advice in this matter in order to make an informed decision given the benefits and risks.

Now, let us consider the analogy of amniotic fluid in the life of every believer. In Christ, we are protected by His blessed flow of life giving power. "He that believeth on me, as the Scripture hath said, out of his belly shall flow rivers of living water" (John 7:38). Oh, Hallelujah! Praise God for His anointing! As our spiritual walk with the Lord develops, we are safe as long as we remain under the ark of safety found in the blood of Jesus. Why does satan so persistently attempt to *draw* us OUT of the protection flowing from our communion with the Holy Spirit? "But every man is tempted, ***when*** he is *drawn* away..." (James 1:14). Satan and every dispatched demon on his payroll aggressively seek to lure us away from that "living water" found in Christ because they have no power in the domain of the Holy Spirit! That's right! The enemy is cast out of heavenly places, so he must *draw* us out to him to wreak havoc in our lives! Don't you remember what happened to Lucifer? In Chapters Four and Seven, we studied the prophet Isaiah's account of Lucifer's fate. He allowed himself to become caught up and kicked OUT! Oh, the enemy knows better than anyone how hazardous it is to step outside the protective arms of God! Now he is slithering and sliding around every corner of the planet looking for another vessel to deceive! Satan is perched on a stoop adjacent to our heart's door with an eighteen gauge needle watching and waiting for his next opportunity to pierce a victim who will hemorrhage to spiritual death. Satan never approaches to heal, but "to steal, kill and destroy" (John 10:10).

Satan can hardly wait to throw his temptation cards out there on his table for the purpose of enticing us away from the Master's table! If we show even the slightest interest in playing satan's game, he is delighted to show us his hand. Beware! As we know every card the enemy holds because his tactics are so predictable, we can be equally assured that he has peeped our hand as well. Satan throws out the first card to swiftly attack our senses (step one), thoughts and mind (step two), imagination (step three), emotions and lusts (step four)! "***When*** lust hath conceived..." (James 1:15). This instant, we must call on the name of the Lord and resist the devil! At the onset of temptation, we would do well to burn rubber back to the peaceful waters near the ark of safety where the protective blood of the Lamb flows richly and powerfully to save us from sin! For if we choose to keep playing the game, satan will not only slap the table in glee, but also slap us around as he goes for the jugular—the kill. Help Lord! The advanced steps of satan's deadly temptation are coming? You KNOW it! He will not stop until we show him our weakened and surrendered will (steps five and six), and then he falls all over himself as he successfully trumps us as "...it bringeth forth sin: and sin, ***when*** it is finished, bringeth forth death" (James 1:15). Believers, we must not take the "***when*** factor" lightly! We can *not* ***WIN*** meeting satan alone at *his* table! The Word admonishes us to resist him! (James 4:7) It's not a question of "if", but "***when***" satan will attack to lure us into his deadly game of temptation! ***When*** we find ourselves in the midst of battle *drawn* dangerously from the ark of safety, knee deep in temptation, remember survival is possible if we quickly draw our Sword of the Spirit on that beast and slay him! The Bible says "he will flee"! (James 4:7) Be steadfast and unmovable when the enemy comes to extract Christ's refreshing, life sustaining fluids from your belly!

Believers make a daily choice (will) to live or die. When threatened physically and spiritually, persons of sound mind, body and soul choose life over death. Only a very troubled individual would knowingly jump in the direct line of a deadly crossfire. Who would jump off a train platform when a steaming locomotive is in view? Would you sign up for a blood drive that made clear its intent to extract every ounce of blood from your body in order to test the results of a lethal injection into your veins? Of course not! But that is exactly what we allow when we sit down to (or more appropriately, lay down prostrate on) satan's table! We surrender our bodies, souls and spirits to the enemy. We allow him to have absolute control over us. Does it make any sense to surrender a life of passionate praise and the invigorating warmth which stems from the glory of God to some loathing snaggle-toothed demon? Of course not! Especially when its sole mission is to capture us, suck all the life out of us by any means necessary and then further infuse our lifeless bodies with embalming fluid corrupt with the deadly substances of the world. Satan daily offers us a fast, but *costly*, ticket from hot, exuberant glorification to cold, steely mortification!! Through Christ, we have the power to tell him NO! Beat it! Scram! Can you ***WIN***? Oh yes! Be Encouraged by His Word! "I can do all things through Christ which strengtheneth me" (Phil. 4:13).

What exactly is spiritual death? Its depth? Its functionality? Its origin? Spiritual death is "the alienation of our beings from the life of God" (Eph. 4:18). Spiritual death is the nature of satan imparted to man through sin. Spiritual death renders man's spirit comatose. The spirit exists, but is alienated or separated from God's Spirit, which is His life. The human spirit exists, but it can neither sense intuitively the movement of God within, nor discern the voice of God from within or without. The human spirit can no longer commune with God because the barrier of sin has wedged its way between its interface with the Holy Spirit. Spiritual death is the cessation or stoppage of communication with God. When a storm arises and knocks down telephone and power lines, communication and energy are temporarily lost, and the broken lines must be repaired before power is restored. When sin was committed in the Garden of Eden, all mankind experienced a turbulent storm that brought down our lines of communication between God and the human spirit. The fall caused a power loss which disabled our ability to turn on the lights, feast on heavenly truths, heat up our houses and turn on our security systems. In other words, the cause and effect of the fall was to flip each switch of our circuits to leave us in total darkness. But thank God for Jesus, who is able to grant complete restoration to those who call on His name.

Spiritual death proliferates more death and mass destruction. Spiritual death precipitates physical death, emotional death, mental death and volitional death. Physical death is the separation of the spirit from the body. When God stops breathing in us, we stop breathing outwardly and that which was of the dust, returns to the dust (Job 33:4; Psalms 104:29). Emotional death is separation and transition of the emotions from desiring, longing for and worshipping God (Genesis

3:6) to desiring, longing for and worshipping satan. Mental death is the separation and transition of our thoughts and ambitions from the will of God to concentrating and focusing thoughts independently on ourselves and our own will for our lives (Psalm 10:4; Prov. 3:5; Isaiah 55:8). Volitional death is deliberate separation of our will from the will of God. It is the separation and elevation of what we choose to do over that which God has predestinated for us to do (Judges 17:6; Prov. 14:12). Volitional death causes man to live, move and act purposelessly.

Spiritual death has its origin in the Garden of Eden when Adam and Eve ate from the forbidden tree (Genesis 3). God forewarned them that if they ate of the tree, they would die (Genesis 2:17). The type of death that God forewarned them of was "spiritual". Physical death resulted from spiritual death, but it was not the initial death referenced in this passage of Scripture. Adam and Eve lived hundreds of years after the fall, which is proof that the initial death spoken of by God to Adam was that of spiritual death. When they ate the fruit of the tree of the knowledge of good and evil, spiritual death was imparted into their beings, injected into their veins and manifested as a side effect in their flesh. They exposed themselves! They exposed their minds! They left their imaginations open to the elements! They laid bare their emotions! They placed their wills out in the open for satan to rule.

The same vicious cycle of temptation and spiritual death occurs today. When we are bombarded with temptation, and allow satan to prevail, our weakened will makes concession with the enemy. The will extracts poison from the world system, fleshly conversations and lustful behavior, and then points the syringe full of vile substance towards the human spirit and injects it into the spirit, releasing death and separation from the only One who has the cure, "Jehovah Rapha, The Lord our Healer"!!

Sin instantly changed man's innocent, god-like nature into the guilty, satanic nature that we are all born with today. When Adam and Eve fell in the garden and spiritual death was imparted, immediately they manifested the effects of being separated from God. Spiritual death takes its toll on our spirit, soul and body and becomes evident through our response system. A change in our attitudes, behavior and lifestyle is noticeable. Disintegration by spiritual death can take place immediately or over extended periods of time, but one thing is for sure, the overt breakdown will happen! Adam and Eve experienced the loss of God-consciousness and the gain of self-consciousness when they saw their own nakedness and attempted to cover it up. Why? Because their conscience, which was God sensitive, turned inward and became self sensitive. Their conscience under conviction gave them a revelation of their new founded, shameful condition. Have you ever noticed the guilt that follows sin? Beware of that bouquet of flowers or those sweet words that closely follow the abusive blows of sin! Adam and Eve cowered as they wallowed in the aftermath of sin. Their eyes were opened so they were able to see that their righteousness was but "filthy rags" (Isaiah 64:6). Their conscience, which called for holiness, suddenly tolerated uncleanness. The garment of God's righteousness became the garment of self and unrighteousness. The wisdom from above that initially brought to their beings purity, peace, easily entreated gentleness and mercy without partiality or hypocrisy, became earthly, sensual and devilish (James 3:15,17). Instead of operating in truth, they began functioning in the nature of satan, the author of lies (John 8:44). Unspeakable joy that filled their hearts and lives turned into excruciating sorrow of heart. The peace that surpassed all understanding became disrupted.

Spiritual death affects the mind and the imagination of all mankind. After the fall, Adam and Eve's thoughts began to roam freely outside of their God-ordained boundaries. The very moment they were alienated from His wisdom, knowledge and understanding, Adam and Eve had to use human intellect to conjure up a remedy for their predicament. As soon as Adam and Eve began operating in spiritual death, they attempted to use unsanctified logic, human ingenuity and brainpower to cover their shame. They endeavored to cover their mistake and attempted to hide their blunder using man made solutions, fig leaves stitched together called "aprons". This blundering "fix-it-yourself" phenomenon caused all in Adam to manifest the same characteristics.

Cain did not use fig leaves to cover up the murder of Abel, but he took him out into the field where he could kill him and leave his body without encountering any known human repercussions (Genesis 4:8). Moses attempted to cover up his killing the Egyptian by hiding him in the depths of the sand (Exodus 2:11-12). David initially attempted to cover up his sin by calling Uriah home from battle so that he could sleep with Bathsheba. When that ploy did not work, he had Uriah placed on the front line of battle to be killed (II Samuel 11).

Remember the issues of sin and guilt brought on by spiritual death? NOT a new report! The shame and the cover up have been going on since the beginning. Adam and Eve, Cain, Moses and David all assumed they had gotten away with their acts only to discover they were caught under the all seeing scope of God's candid camera! The God who never slumbers nor sleeps saw them! The God who ponders all of man's comings and goings caught them in the very act. Of course, we still attempt to cover up our errors, faults and imperfections today. Oh yes, we feel more sophisticated in our approach, but God is still omniscient and omnipresent. We *think* we can hide behind the walls of hotel rooms and cover up the pregnancy by having an abortion. Can you recall scandals where paper shredders were used to cut up confidential documents critical to highly visible cases? We use alibis, "scapegoats" and "fall guys" to cover up the truth or pass the blame, but we must not be fooled. God knows the true culprit!

Spiritual death manifests itself in the form of vulnerability and fear. Imagine our peace in Christ being totally shaken. That alone is enough to terrify anybody! Adam and Eve feared the Lord God who they walked and talked with in the cool of the garden. They feared the Master of all creation—the One who loved and cared for them and supplied their every need! After sin, spiritual death ushered in a completely different fear. A cold and gripping fear seized Adam and Eve's emotions and handcuffed their feelings at the scene of the crime! Before sin, Adam and Eve heard the loving voice of God as music to their ears. After the fall, God's voice literally terrified their hearts as the heavenly atmosphere became electrified with fear and they suddenly heard His voice of judgment pass sentence against them. The Garden of peace and repose vanished into thin air and became a garden of chaotic unrest.

Fear continues to grip and freeze mankind. If satan can isolate us from the Spirit of God and keep us running sideways, backwards and off balance in fear, he has dominion over us! Abram operated in fear, not once, but twice, when he had Sarai to lie about her relationship to him (Genesis 12:11-13; 20:2). Similarly, Isaac operated in fear when he lied to Abimelech about Rebekah's status as his wife, calling her his sister (Genesis 26:7). The ten spies operated in fear after viewing the promise land, choosing to see themselves as grasshoppers instead of overcomers (Numbers 13:33). Thousands of Gideon's men broke ranks with him because they operated in fear (Judges 7:3). These are only a few Biblical representations of individuals operating in fear. Opportunities to operate in fear are presented to us daily, and fear vexes our decision making process just as frequently. The fear of walking in the dark troubles more souls than we would ever desire to acknowledge. The fear of the unknown complicates the broadcast for our futures. The fear of the loss in finances affects our willingness to share and to spend. Fear is the manifestation of the human spirit disconnected with the Spirit of God! Lord, please remind us that You said in Your Word "For God hath not given us the spirit of fear; but of power, and of love and of a sound mind"! (II Timothy 1:7) Hallelujah!

Spiritual death not only affects man, but also the ground, animals, vegetation and the entire world. Prior to sin, Adam tilled the ground without any difficulty. He named the animals, grew healthy vegetation, and the world was a glimpse of heaven (Genesis 2:5, 9,10-14,19, 20). When sin entered the world, death by sin reversed the divine order of God and blessings upon mankind, the animals, the vegetation and the world, and cursed them with a curse (Genesis 3: 14-19). The Bible teaches us that, "wherefore, as by one man sin entered into this world, and death by sin; and so death passed upon all men, for that all have sinned" (Romans 5:12). It was through the fall of man or by one man's disobedience that we were made sinners (Romans 5:19) and infected with the virus called spiritual death. A virus is contagious, infectious and transmittable. What a catastrophe! Look at this picture! Man laid down on the "cooling board" or the coroner's slab and allowed the enemy to drain him of God's life. "For the life of the flesh is in the blood..." (Lev. 17:11). Man allowed himself to be embalmed with the venomous fluid flowing from satan's veins. The human spirit, once quickened by the Holy Spirit, and marked by a rich blood flow circulating freely throughout man's entire being, bringing life and energy to do God's will, is now destroyed by sin. The spiritually lifeless man is completely overcome by the nature and power of satan to do his will and everything humanly possible against the will of God. God help us to avoid falling into temptation, sin, spiritual death and destruction!

This process of withdrawing from the world, (worldly people, environments and things) and administering or injecting them into our beings, takes place all day everyday and we do not even realize how and when it happens. We allow satan to teach us to inject ourselves with his poison as a junkie injects himself with drugs. We too often permit openings for deadly habits that give birth to strongholds that keep us from realizing our purpose in life and fulfilling our purpose in Christ. When spiritual death is released into our beings and hearts, it begins to negatively impact and affect the response system of all members of our bodies. That is, when our members are not energized by the life of God, they no longer respond to the voice of God, nor the Spirit of God. Remember the human heart circulates oxygenated and deoxygenated blood through the members of the body. Whenever a component part of the body fails to receive oxygenated blood, it begins to die and wither away. The dysfunctionality of the organ or member is marked by discoloration, fever, loss of mobility, weakness, etc.

This analogy is true in the spirit realm as well. When our spiritual heart fails to circulate the blood of God from our hearts through our arteries to our members, the blockage causes a response failure to the commands of God. When the blood of God does not travel through our being, we might experience chills one moment and a high pitched fever the next! We don't know whether to respond with a frigid shoulder or flare up in a hot fit of tempered rage. When the blood of God does not pass through our spirits, souls and bodies, we become discolored as if we have seen a ghost, instead of looking like Moses when he came out of the mountain after spending time with Jehovah (Exodus 34:29-35). When the life of God does not move through our wills, we become weak, frail and vulnerable to temptations as were the children of Israel (Exodus 32:1-6). When our hearts are not properly nourished with the life of God, we become hardened, blind, insensitive, evil, devising wicked imaginations (Prov. 6:18) instead of offering hope to those in need (I Peter 3:15). When the life of God does not flow to our hands, we do not desire to lift up holy hands before God as an evening sacrifice (Psalms 141:2), but we allow them to be used to shed innocent blood (Prov. 6:17). When the life and power of God do not surge into our feet, we do not choose to dance with all our might before the Lord as King David (II Samuel 6:14), but we find our feet swiftly running to mischief (Prov. 6:18). When the Source of our strength does not wash upon the shores of our tongue, we do not speak words of life, hope and healing (Prov. 18:21), but instead we let corrupt communications spew out of our mouths. Off of our tongues flow words that do not edify, but tell lies and sow discord (Eph. 4:29; Prov. 6:17,19). Paul was led to write and speak these alarming words to the Church at Rome, "Neither yield ye your members as instruments of unrighteousness unto sin: but yield yourselves unto God, as those that are alive from the dead, and your members as instruments of righteousness unto God" (Romans 6:13). Believers at the Church in Rome struggled tremendously. They had trouble appropriately responding to God. There was confusion because they behaved as if their members were still disconnected from the life of God. They did not understand or had difficulty accepting the fact that they had within them the power, nature and life of God (if they so chose to yield to it). How many of us struggle with these same issues today? How many of us have the power of God flowing through certain members of our bodies while other members are still operating in spiritual death? If the truth be told, everyone of us has a member or members in which the life of God has not touched, or if it has quickened us, we choose to be selfish and have it our way! Believers, we have a daily struggle. If we yield our members to God, we will enjoy the overflow of His blessings on our lives!

As we have studied the course of satan's eight deadly steps in temptation, we should now find the cycle identifiable and predictable. With the help of the Lord, we should also know that the worst outcomes are preventable. We have learned the advantages of resisting the devil and his devices *before* he is well into the advanced stages of the temptation process. After all, it is usually easier to control and "nip in the bud" what we receive through our senses than it is to survive the tremendous pressure generated by the ***combination*** of our stimulated senses (step 1), our thoughts and imaginations running wild under the influence of satan (steps 2 and 3), and our emotionally stirred up lusts (step 4) beating heavily against our weakening will (step 5)! The "domino effect" is *rough*! We now KNOW that surrendering our will to satan (step 6) guarantees the commitment of sin (step 7), and where there is sin, there is spiritual death (step 8).

Believers, isn't it good to know we have hope? What would be the point of learning all about satan's steps of temptation if there were no way to defeat him and his demons of destruction? Oh, praise God that we are not bound and shackled by sin! Believers who prevail against the wiles of satan enjoy the reward of salvation and sweet communion with Christ. We remain dedicated to exposing satan's methods so we can bring down every stronghold against us. Is temptation certain? Yes. Must we fail? **No**!

> "Now unto him that is able to *keep* you from falling, and to present you faultless before the presence of his glory with exceeding joy, To the only wise God our Saviour, be glory and majesty, dominion and power, both now and ever. Amen." (Jude 1:24,25)

ABOUT THE AUTHOR

Elder Ralph Anthony Martino is an ordained preacher, Biblical teacher, evangelist, motivational speaker, workshop facilitator, and entrepreneur.

He is the pastor of the First Church of Christ (Hol.) U.S.A., located at 1219 Hamlin Street, N.E., Washington, D.C.

He possesses a B.S. in Business Administration and a Masters in Religious Education. He is a Biblical Expositor, who ministers the word of God from a holistic viewpoint (spirit, soul, and body). He ministers weekly to believers from diverse cultures and denominations. The passion GOD birth within him for the Word of GOD and the desire to see believers experience healing, deliverance and prosperity compels him to share and communicate the engrafted Word of GOD, which is able to save the soul.

He is married to a virtuous woman, Vondrenna Douglas-Martino, and they are the blessed parents of two daughters: Olivia Janey Martino and Elizabeth Alexia Martino.

To contact the author for workshops, seminars, speaking engagements or puchasing books or tapes, please call or write:

Elder Ralph A. Martino
Watch and Pray Ministries
P.O. Box 1101
Lanham, MD 20706
1 (800) 436-5826

Or email:

www.watchandprayministries.com